CAN'T YOU TALK LOUDER, GOD?

*Secrets to **Hearing** the **Voice** of God*

2nd Edition
Revised and Updated

Steve Shultz

Can't You Talk Louder, God?
© Copyright 2015 – Steve Shultz
Revised and Updated 2nd Edition, 2015

All rights reserved.

This book is protected by the copyright laws of the United States of America. This book may not be copied or reprinted for commercial gain or profit. The use of short quotations or occasional page copying for personal or group study is permitted and encouraged. Permission will be granted upon request. Unless otherwise identified, Scripture quotations are from the HOLY BIBLE, NEW INTERNATIONAL VERSION, Copyright © 1973, 1978, 1984, by International Bible Society. Used by permission of Zondervan Publishing House.

Please note that Elijah List Publication's publishing style capitalizes certain pronouns in Scripture that refer to the Father, Son, and Holy Spirit, and may differ from some publishers' styles. Also the name satan and related names are not capitalized. We choose not to acknowledge him, even to the point of us violating grammatical rules.

ELIJAH LIST PUBLICATIONS, LLC
528 Ellsworth St. SW, Albany, OR 97321 USA

"The lion has roared—who will not fear? The Sovereign Lord has spoken—who can but prophesy?" Amos 3:8

This book and all other Elijah List Publications products and resources are available online at our webstore at **www.elijahshopper.com**.

For more information, call us at **541-926-3250** or **866-354-5245** or send us an email at: **info@elijahlist.net**. Or reach us on the Internet: **www.elijahlist.com**.

ISBN 978-1-938311-19-2
Printed in the United States.
For Worldwide Distribution.
1 2 3 4 5 6 7 8 9 10 11 / 10 05 15

Managing Editor: Julie A. Smith
Cover design and editor: Tawny Nelson

DEDICATION

To Derene, my wife, my best friend,
and the mother of our three grown children.

Without you, Derene, as my life partner,
nothing would have made life this good!

ACKNOWLEDGEMENTS

As with any book, there are more thank yous to be said than there is room to say them. But I will name a few of the more prominent ones I wish to acknowledge, I first want to thank the Lord, our Savior Jesus Christ, whose VOICE this book is all about.

Because of the patient understanding of my wife and children through all my sitting and typing, when sometimes I did not even "hear" the questions they asked of me, I want to say, "Thank you, Derene, Tawny, Danielle, and Christopher." I love you!

I also want to acknowledge some of the most prominent among my helpers, advisors in life, intercessors both life long and current, and to some prophetic intercessors and prophets who my gratitude goes out to:

Chuck D. Pierce, Doug Addison, James Goll, Denny Cramer, Kim Clement, Jane Hamon, Dutch Sheets, Dr. Alveda King, Joan Hunter, Dr. James Maloney, John Mark Pool, Kim Alexis, Lana Vawser, Jennifer Eivaz, Dr. Paul and Donna Cox, Tammy Kling, Joseph Keesling, Dr. Mathai and Mariama Mathai, Tawny Nelson, Julie A. Smith, Dawn Baker, Pat Ferguson, Nancy Taylor, Persis Tiner, Ramona Mathany, Jay West, Sandy and Rick Gales, Lisa and Charles Doyle, Dennis and Cathy Wilhelm, Mike and Lori Salley, JD and Charlotte Hadley, Emiko Soon, and of course, my pastor and friend, Denny Cline, and his wife, Ann, to name just a few of the many who have carried me in prayer.

And finally, my heartfelt thanks to the entire Elijah List Team, especially Dennis and Cathy Wilhelm, and my editorial team Julie A. Smith and Tawny Nelson.

ENDORSEMENTS

With *Can't You Talk Louder, God?* Steve Shultz continues in his passionate pursuit to help the Body of Christ to know God's voice. In learning how to recognize the voice of God, Steve shows how every person open to hearing God can affect the world around them. This very practical, yet inspirational, book encourages readers to step confidently into their destiny in Christ.

Bill Johnson, Senior Pastor
Bethel Church
Redding, California

I don't know of another person on the face of the earth at this time in church history who has engaged in networking prophetic ministries and releasing prophetic directives as much as Steve Shultz.Today, through the Elijah List, millions of people are introduced to current, valid, prophetic revelation through prophets—some very visible and others obscure. Steve walks in some of the highest degrees of prophetic integrity that I have personally witnessed and his book, *Can't You Talk Louder, God?* is filled with the treasures of his journey in hearing the voice of God. His heart is for the whole Body to know Heaven's voice...and that is why the Lord has entrusted Steve with the gift to influence those in the whole wide world who are hungry for the true, pure prophetic voice of the Lord. *Can't You Talk Louder, God?* will open up realms of insight, revelation, and confidence in hearing God's voice.

Patricia King
Extreme Prophetic

CONTENTS

Foreword by James W. Goll..11

Chapter 1.....Did God Really Say...?..15

Chapter 2.....What If Jesus Told You He Enjoyed
Your Daily Chats Together?........................27

Chapter 3.....My Sheep Hear My Voice..31

Chapter 4.....Today, When You Hear His Voice............................39

Chapter 5.....You Can't Stop God; He's Already Speaking..........47

Chapter 6.....Divine Appointments—A Way to Listen to God...59

Chapter 7.....Does God Speak Through the Bible—or
Only Teach?..73

Chapter 8....."Pineapple Theology"..77

Chapter 9.....God's Voice—What Does It Actually
Sound Like?..83

Chapter 10.....Have You Gone "Compelling" Lately?...................89

Chapter 11.....Hearing God Speak Through
Your "Father Filter"..101

Chapter 12.....Hearing vs. Obeying God's Voice.........................111

Chapter 13.....God—Just How Busy Is He?.................................115

Chapter 14....."How Good Do I Have to Be to
                Hear God's Voice?"................................121

Chapter 15....."How Bad Do I Have to Be for
                God to Stop Talking to Me?"..................127

Chapter 16.....Dreams, a Way to Hear God's Voice....................131

Chapter 17.....When They Tell You God Doesn't
                Speak Today..137

Chapter 18.....Debugging the Prophetic...141

Conclusion.....Have You NOTICED? God Is TALKING
                LOUDER NOW?...153

FOREWORD BY
JAMES W. GOLL

Does God play games with His kids? Of course, He does! I totally believe this and that is why the volume switch is on His end and not yours! Up and down the volume level goes. Real time experience goes something like this: real loud to deafening soft. And seemingly not much between! Zooming in and out with His telescopic lens, the Holy Spirit creates close encounters and yes, far away ones. He is great at games like hide and seek, you're hot—you're cold—you're getting closer... In my walk with Him I have learned that He is the Master, and He wants to be in charge of your learning curve!

"My sheep hear My voice, I know them and they follow Me." This verse from John 10:27 is the hallmark verse that my journey in learning to hear and obey His endearing voice has been centered on. Perhaps it will be in your life as well.

When I was a college student way back in 1972, I was filled and rather saturated with the Holy Spirit through encounters with the wild, radical, and yes, crazy Jesus People. Life was new and my little black and white TV set switched channels to omnicolor vision overnight. I wanted all that the Lord Jesus Christ had to offer.

One late night a friend and I went to a church near our college campus that happened to be open. A single candle in the sanctuary was lit representing the presence of the Holy Spirit. There we kneeled in prayer dedicating ourselves to Christ's service. I opened my Bible and read the verse in John about hearing His voice.

I made a pragmatic deal with God that night. I told Him, "I have no problem with the fact that I am Your sheep. I have accepted Jesus as my Lord; He is my Shepherd and I am Your sheep." I added, "And I really do not have a problem at all with the truth that You know me. I know that You know me." I went on with my rather logical presentation, "I even accept by faith that I do hear Your voice. I have heard and felt You knocking at the door of my heart—so I accept that I do hear Your voice." I continued in my prayerful arguing posture, "But I have a problem with the rest of this verse, 'they follow Me.' I want to follow You. Here's the deal God, I hear more than just Your voice! I hear the voice of the world, my flesh, the enemy of darkness at times, and Yours mixed in as well. I need some help! If I am really going to follow You, then I must do more than just hear Your voice, I must discern it from the other voices."

I knelt in prayer that fabled night and asked Him to enroll me in His "school of hearing and discerning" the voice of the Holy Spirit. I encourage you to do the same. It worked for me. It can work for you.

Today, yes, more than four decades later, a lot of things have changed. Today we have actual Schools of the Spirit, conferences, training centers, and equipping materials to aid us in our walk with Him. Imagine the difference from the mid 1970s and today. In my day, the cassette tape was being introduced! Today we have the Internet—an amazing and valuable source of information at our finger tips. Today we have creative tools in the media and e-resources like THE ELIJAH LIST sending out teaching and training to the growing prophetic community. It is truly amazing!

Sitting in your hands is another great tool for such a time as this. It is another installment in God's "School of the Spirit." Having appreciated and walked with Steve Shultz now for many years, I can vouch for his integrity in his life and ministry, and the many practical messages that he brings.

One of Steve's goals is to demystify the prophetic—or the art of hearing and following the voice of God. Steve and his team aptly call it "Debugging the Prophetic." Good terms. Good goals. And a job well done!

Yes, God wants you to hear His voice more than you want to hear it! He really does! And this book, right in your very hands, will help you learn lessons from one of God's best students. Take and eat lessons from the trenches from another of God's listening servants.

Dr. James W. Goll
Encounters Network
Author of *The Seer, Dream Language, The Lost Art of Intercession, Praying for Israel's Destiny, Angelic Encounters,* and others.

CHAPTER 1
DID GOD REALLY SAY...?

Satan Is "In Your Face." God Is "Behind You."

Since the Garden of Eden, satan has confronted man—to his face! His question—his accusation—has always been, "Did God *really* say that?" Casting aspersions on the validity of God's Word, he seeks to create doubt in what God has said.

And now satan is lying to the Church again, in a very big way. His accusation is that God isn't speaking to His Church at all anymore—other than what was written 2,000 years ago. And millions have believed this lie. Even many theologians say that since the time when the Bible was written, God went deaf and mute. They explain, "He only speaks through the written Word." This lie has been spread to many churches—from Baptist to Pentecostal!

Just remember, in-your-face *doubt* is the devil's specialty.

The problem in the Garden of Eden was that there was *some* truth in satan's accusation against God that he gave to Eve on that day. God really *did* say *some* of what satan claimed. Satan, who Jesus called, "the father of lies," and "a liar from the beginning," knew the ropes regarding how to lead people into deception, and he still does today.

Satan first claimed to Adam and Eve that God's problem was that He knew if they ate of the Tree of the Knowledge of Good and Evil, they would become like Him. That part was *actually true*. God even admitted it a bit later in the story.

The serpent twisted and contorted what he knew to be the truth. What he said *contained* truth, but it was not "truth*ful*." It wasn't *full* of truth. Embedded in his words were seeds of innuendos and subtle deceptions.

*"You will not surely die," the serpent said to the woman. "For God knows that when you eat of it your eyes will be opened, and **you will be like God, knowing good and evil**"* (Genesis 3:4-5, emphasis added).

After the Fall, God confirmed satan's statement: *"And the LORD God said, **'The man has now become like one of us, knowing good and evil**. He must not be allowed to reach out his hand and take also from the tree of life and eat, and live forever'"* (Genesis 3:22, emphasis added).

Satan Talks Up a Storm

Satan is not terribly creative. He never stops talking; all the while convincing much of the Church that God Himself has completely *stopped* talking.

Satan is still saying, "Has God really said that? Is God really talking to you?" Satan continues, "Or has He pulled back, because He still doesn't want you to become like Him?"

Because of satan's incessant accusations, it is critical that you understand one of his favorite lies of all time—that God is not talking to you—*at all*!

But the Good News: God is still talking!

Satan snarls, "God *is* way too busy with the things of the universe and the world to talk to little ol' you!" If he can get you to believe this lie, he has won the battle. He knows that he will be in deep trouble if people ever discover how to consistently and clearly hear God's voice. So, he must keep them from believing that God wants to talk to them directly *and personally*.

And far too many Christians believe it. Direct from the pit of hell, this lie is repeated and yet, by the millions, it sounds so credible that "believers" no longer actually *believe* that God is alive and well and *is*, Himself, talking up a storm to *them*.

This book is written to expose that lie—to expose it to every Christian of every denomination.

Many Christians I've spoken to, who have tried to convince me that God *doesn't* speak to people today, except through Scripture, are the same Christians who, by one method or another, teach their own children and friends that God *does* indeed speak!

Confused? You should be. Those Christians are confused and they don't even know it. While protesting that God doesn't speak today, they'll say things like, "I just felt like I should call Joe, for some reason." Or, "I had an impression that I should go visit my aunt today."

If you press them about this point, as I have, most will end up admitting that God was somehow encouraging them to do something. This represents quite a contradiction. He doesn't speak—but then, He does speak, doesn't He?

Much of what you read in these pages will begin to clarify and make exciting the possibilities that, if these thoughts and impressions are indeed from God, then what more might be out there from God that *He wants to say to me*?

God Speaks and the Storm Is Calmed

Satan talks up a storm. But God speaks in the storm. God shows up, speaks daily, and calms the storms that are created by satan.

Let's repeat the good news about God. He is still talking—and He's talking to *you*—all of the time!

Oddly enough, most Christians actually, somewhere deep inside, know that it's not only *the* holy written Word of God that is spoken (which of course is the standard by which everything else must be judged). At a heart level, most groan for more communication with God that they sense other Christians have. They long for a *personal* word from God.

When we were saved, weren't we promised, after all, a *personal* relationship with God?

We all want our revelation to become more alive and real, vibrant, moving, changeless, yet ever creative. Most of us know it's there, yet we grasp with all that is within us to realize—in our experience—what the old songs have claimed all along!

> I serve a risen Savior, He's in the world today;
> I know that He is living, whatever men may say,
> I see His hand of mercy, **I hear His voice** of cheer,
> And **just the time I need Him, He's always near.**
>
> He lives, He lives, Christ Jesus lives today!
> **He walks with me and talks with me
> along life's narrow way.**
> He lives, He lives, salvation to impart!
> You ask me how I know He lives? He
> lives within my heart.

("He Lives" by Alfred H. Ackley. Copyright 1933 by Homer Rodeheaver. Copyright Renewed 1961, The Rodeheaver Co., owner. All rights reserved.)

See what I mean?

Another great hymn that many of us have sung since childhood is "In the Garden."

> I come to the garden alone,
> While the dew is still on the roses;
> And the voice I hear, falling on my ear,

The Son of God discloses.

And He walks with me, and He talks with me,
And He tells me I am His own;
And the joy we share as we tarry there,
None other has ever known.
He **speaks**, and the **sound of His voice**
Is so sweet the birds hush their singing,
And the melody that He gave to me
Within my heart is ringing.

("In the Garden" by C. Austin Miles.
Copyright 1912 by Hall-Mack Co.
Copyright renewal 1940, extended.
The Rodeheaver Co., owner. All rights reserved.)

God, from the beginning, has been actively involved in the business of proving to mankind that He is alive! He wants us to know what He really is saying and *has been* saying—and *continues* to say. Doesn't it make sense that God would want to communicate His will and purposes to His people? Communication is at the heart of all relationships. How could there be a deep, personal relationship with God if there is no communication?

The confusing part is that the Church, as a whole, has believed that He is alive, but at the same time, the Church has been clueless as to what God is up to. What *is* He up to if He is not speaking?

Let me tell you the answer to that question. He's up to good things for you personally and daily in your life. He rejoices over you with singing, and He calls you His friend. He longs to converse with you, not just with words on a page, but as the Love of your life.

So What Does He Sound Like?

Sometimes God holds Himself back, almost hiding Himself because, as one pastor put it, "He wants you to chase Him until He catches you!"

It is the glory of God to conceal a thing: but the honour of kings is to search out a matter (Proverbs 25:2 KJV).

He may reveal Himself as that *"still small voice"* (1 Kings 19:12 KJV). He is the One who must be carefully discerned and sought after with all your heart—to know His will. *"But if from thence thou shalt seek the LORD thy God, thou shalt find Him, if thou seek Him with all thy heart and with all thy soul"* (Deuteronomy 4:29 KJV).

*And after the earthquake a fire; but the LORD was not in the fire: and after the fire **a still small voice*** (1 Kings 19:12 KJV, emphasis added).

And yet, at other times, He shows Himself in thunderings. *"The people therefore, that stood by, and heard it, **said that it thundered"*** (John 12:29 KJV, emphasis added). Still, at other times He is to you the Creator who says, "You have not because you *ask not*" (James 4:2, author's paraphrase). He who wants to have a special and personal relationship with you, needs you to seek Him for it:

Henceforth I call you not servants; for the servant knoweth not what his lord doeth: but I have called you friends; for all things that I have heard of My Father I have made known unto you (John 15:15 KJV).

In His personal story, Jesus' mother, Mary, appears to "ambush" her own Son at a wedding party one day. I love that Jesus' ministry started at a celebration with rejoicing. He is *our* Bridegroom, is He not? Sometimes great things happen in very unusual places—even at weddings.

"God with skin on"—Jesus—claiming that His time had not yet come, was there with His mother at the wedding. Perhaps Mary had heard the Father's voice tell her something that morning. Perhaps Jesus was just testing her level of belief when He refused to help her at first. This would *not* be the last time He would first pretend to refuse to help and then would later give that help. (Later in His ministry, Jesus would pretend not to help the woman at Tyre, for example. But, when He had tested her faith, He instantly healed her daughter.)

But this *is* for sure what happened at the wedding party in Cana: Jesus' mother, after telling Jesus that the wine was gone, said to the servants, *"Do whatever He tells you"*(John 2:5). God is still saying, "If you listen and do what I tell you to do, things will go so much better for you! You'll be like a house built on the solid Rock, if you'll just hear and do what I'm telling you to do."

My goodness! He loves to talk to people! If you think satan is an incessant talker, he has nothing on the Father, the Son, and the Holy Spirit! They are the Ones who created talking in the first place. And they never stop talking—the Holy Spirit quite literally lives inside you.

This Is Your Situation

I can state what your situation is as a fact, because it is everyone's situation. Everyone hears the lying voice of the enemy. Everyone!

Satan is always in your face, like a roaring lion—*lying*. He is always asking you, "Did God *really* say that to you?" Or, "Aren't you just making that up in your mind—those words that you feel God is speaking to you? Aren't those times you felt God speak to you, just your vivid imagination at work?"

Meanwhile, God, the other kind of Lion, the Lion of Judah, comes to you in whatever fashion He chooses: as thunder, or in the still, small voice, in a vision, or a simple impression; in Scripture, or in a dream in the night. He waits, usually patiently (but not always patiently), to be invited into your mind, your thoughts, your heart, and your life.

Once "inside," however—once you finally believe, not only that He speaks, but also that He wants to speak to *you*— He's got you! You're addicted. Because God *is* the ultimate "addiction." The more He talks, the more you want to hear Him talk. You become addicted to the sound of His voice.

Every other addiction in the world is the enemy's cheap substitute for being addicted to God. He's the One to whom the Scripture refers when it says, *"Whether you turn to the right or to the left,* ***your ears will hear a voice behind you****, saying, 'This is the way; walk in it'"* (Isaiah 30:21, emphasis added).

Why Is He Behind You?

Why does God represent Himself as a voice *behind* you?

Is it because He's difficult to hear? No, it's not that at all, because sometimes, as we've said, He's loud! Then why do the Scriptures talk about the voice behind you?

> *On the Lord's Day I was in the Spirit, and I heard* **behind me a loud voice** *like a trumpet, which said: "Write on a scroll what you see and send it to the seven churches…"*
> (Revelation 1:10-11, emphasis added).

I fervently believe that He is the voice behind you, because *He's got your back covered.*

In His Word He tells you that He sees the unseen. He knows the location of every demon at every moment on earth, 24 hours a day, and *He's got your back covered.* He's guiding you with His eye to help you avoid peril and pitfalls.

And since He can see that which we cannot see—ought we not to listen closely to His voice and learn to hear it better? Wouldn't that be an improvement over satan's lie, which tells us that God isn't even speaking today?

But, beware—if satan knows that you are settled and believe that God is actually alive and speaking today, his lie has to change to this: satan whispers, "God certainly doesn't have time for your *puny*, little problems. Look at all the suffering in the world!" The devil says, "Why should God care about your car or your house or your healthy child?" Satan adapts his lies to our situations, as he seeks to continue to prevent us from listening to God.

Satan's Big Fear

Satan doesn't want you to hear God's voice. Why? Because you will be quickly transformed by it, and the enemy is scared to death about your potential transformation, because the more you are transformed, the more you will become an infectious Christian.

But worse, it is inevitable that, over time, you will continue to be even *more* transformed. Faster and faster, from glory to glory, because the more you hear, the more you'll want to hear from Heaven—and satan is shaking in his boots about that.

How do I know?

It's in the Word, as evidenced in the first miracle Jesus ever performed. At that wedding party in Cana, Jesus was painting a word picture on the canvas of our hearts and minds to demonstrate His priorities toward sinful and wounded people—the ones He died for.

"What painting is that?" you ask.

Nearby stood six stone water jars, the kind used by the Jews for ceremonial washing, each holding from twenty to thirty gallons (John 2:6).

It's fascinating to me that 20-30 gallons is the rough volume of the human body. (I know because I calculated it based on the fact that 60-70 percent of the human body is composed of water).

And even a casual study of the Word teaches that "six" represents the number of man. Jesus was making a point here. God told Mary to tell Jesus to fill six stone-cold, empty, dirty, water jars—the "kind used for ceremonial washing." I believe that each jar seems to represent filthy, dried up, set-off-to-the-side, or abused people. In other words, you and me.

As humankind, we find ourselves standing in all our filth. We are the ceremonial pots and legalistic rituals, and Jesus wants to transform us into the best wine that was saved for last. Wherever believers are caught in *traditions*, the Lord wants to transform us and make us ready for exciting adventures. He even claims in the Word, that those who know their God will do great exploits! (See Daniel 11:32.)

Some Will Be Jolted and Some Simply Awakened!

God is upon you in this hour (or you wouldn't be reading this book), and you are about to be jolted awake.

Dr. Richard E. Eby in his book *Caught Up into Paradise* relates this story. "One Scientist, decades ago, the father of Dr. Richard E. Eby, tirelessly and for many years worked on an electrical insulator (called a "bushing") for G.E. This bushing needed to be made to carry enough voltage to transfer electricity over long distances from Boulder Dam. No such insulator had ever succeeded."

The White House and the then President Hoover urged the senior Mr. Eby to solve this problem in a hurry. Eby nearly gave up and he told God so, just before falling asleep one night. The next morning, Mr Eby's Bible opened to the story of the Wedding at Cana. Eby felt strongly impressed by God it would indeed take millions of volts to transform water into wine at CANA. In fact, God questioned him that day, "Did I not use 6 pots? Big ones? Was it not My power that changed the water?" One thing led to another and one of Eby's team member's shortly took a trip, finding some middle-eastern pottery in Egypt. Eby told him to make a "bushing" (or insulator) out of the same formula of this pottery he had found. The problem was solved and Boulder Dam could now become a reality. The rest is history.

For some of you who are reading these words right now and seeking to hear God's voice better than you already do, this book will be less of a jolt to your paradigm of understanding, but it will be for you a fresh jump-start, an awakening, if you will, into the transformation of your inner man. The more awakened you become to God's desire to talk to you, the greater will be your desire to pursue every avenue that opens up to hear His voice.

And God loves a great pursuit! This book contains help for you to hear His voice for the first time—or to hear it better and better until the end of time. And, through it, some of you will begin to grasp—perhaps for the first time—that you've been hearing His voice your entire life! You just didn't recognize it.

With new revelation that will come through Scriptures and stories, you will most certainly begin to hear His voice better than you currently do. You will even begin to hear His voice "on purpose" instead of by accident. And you will learn to tune in to God's voice.

He is the voice behind you—He's standing in the background. But He is continually speaking to you. And yes, you are hearing Him, whether you've realized it or not—all along!

It matters not if you are a Baptist, a Pentecostal, or "Bapticostal"—you've all been hearing His voice since you were born.

You're just getting warmed up!

I feel like saying, "Ladies and gentlemen, start your engines!"

CHAPTER 2

WHAT IF JESUS TOLD YOU HE ENJOYED YOUR DAILY CHATS TOGETHER?
(THE CHATS YOU DIDN'T EVEN KNOW YOU WERE HAVING.)

What if you and I were talking over lunch and you protested, as many have to me, that you don't hear God's voice as well as others do—or you may even insist that God doesn't speak at all. And if He does, He certainly doesn't speak to you.

And then, what if I not only insisted—as one who lives this "stuff—that you *do* hear God's voice, and you have, in fact, *been* hearing His voice clearly for a very long time—for your entire life?

Picture then—instead of *me* telling you this—Jesus walks up to our table, surprises us both and says directly and lovingly to you, "I just wanted to thank you for all the talks you and I have had together. I look forward to them every day!"

"But, Jesus, I don't ever hear your voice," you would protest, embarrassingly.

Then the Savior replies, "Not only do you hear My voice, but we have some of the most wonderful chats Heaven has ever heard! For such a time as this you were born; so you and I could talk, like we do, *all* the time while you are here on earth."

"Impossible!" you might insist, because you may feel that Jesus' statement is difficult or even impossible to grasp, and certainly too good to be true.

But, honestly, it is simply too biblical to ignore.

Think of how the disciples must have felt when Jesus told

them in their Galilean lingo, "*I used to call you a servant, but a master doesn't confide in his servants. But since you received Me, **I call you My friend. That's why I've been telling you everything the Father tells Me.**"* (Paraphrased from John 15:15, emphasis added).

The disciples had the benefit of seeing "God with skin on" in the person of the Son of God, Jesus Christ. But most of the time they didn't fully understand who He was. They saw Him, touched Him, and heard His voice, yet they never fully grasped what and who Jesus really was, until He ascended to Heaven.

On the other hand, you, in hindsight, *know* who Jesus is, yet you don't get to walk around with Him. Instead, you received more! He lives in you. Doesn't the Bible say you are the temple of the Holy Spirit?

Do you not know that your body is a temple of the Holy Spirit, who is in you, whom you have received from God? You are not your own (1 Corinthians 6:19 NIV).

Your challenge is different than the disciples' challenge. Your challenge is to finally grasp, once and for all, that since He lives in you, you cannot help but hear Him—that is, it's simply impossible *not* to hear Him speak. Since you are an inhabited creation that is inhabited by God, the Holy Spirit, how can you not hear Him speak?

Of course, Jesus always knew this would sound too unbelievably good to be true, so He had it recorded emphatically in His Word. He knew we would need reminding. That way there could be no question for those who are willing to accept this "easy" truth that is sometimes "hard" to believe.

Jesus said, "***My sheep listen (recognize) My voice;*** *I know them, and they follow Me*" (John 10:27 NLT, emphasis added).

The last I checked, you and I are still the sheep of His pasture, and He is still the "Good Shepherd."

If He is the Shepherd and you are the sheep, it doesn't make much difference what you believe—as least as far as facts are concerned. The fact is, you recognize (or hear clearly) His voice, and you've recognized it all along—even though you didn't think you did. This is a simple biblical truth.

You might say, "But, that's not logical!"

To which Jesus would reply, "No, but it is *theological*—that is, it's God-logical!"

What About Those Talks?

You've been talking to Him, and He's been talking to you. Perhaps now you can begin to grasp that He's been talking to you. But what about the fact that you have supposedly been talking to Him? Maybe you have felt faithless and failing in your prayers? How is it then that He hears you talking to Him?

Even the Old Testament Scriptures are not silent about how God sees you and how He knows your thoughts. Read what David wrote, incredulously, to God:

> *You know when I sit and when I rise;*
> **You perceive my thoughts from afar.**
>
> *You discern my going out and my lying down;*
> *You are familiar with all my ways.*
>
> **Before a word is on my tongue**
> **You know it completely, O LORD.**
>
> *Such knowledge is too wonderful for me,*
> *too lofty for me to attain.*
> (Psalm 139:2-4, 6, emphasis added)

Even those of you who have shed great tears because of the tragedies in your life and the mistakes you have made, nevertheless you have been speaking to God; and a reward for your tears is promised.

"Those who sow in tears will reap with songs of joy" (Psalm 126:5). Your tears are one of the ways you talk to God! They are expressions of your deepest emotion directed toward Him.

All you have to do now is "deal with it." You've been having two-way conversations with God, listening and obeying (and sometimes choosing not to obey) His voice for a long time.

Now, having come to grips with this amazing truth, why not learn to hear Him even better by listening to His voice? Many of you have been hearing Him and not knowing it. What would happen if you accepted this fact and started to tune in to His voice more intentionally? We now know that before a word is on our tongues, He knows it; all our days are planned and we are His sheep; and His sheep do, in fact, listen to His voice. So now, why not start listening to Jesus talk to you and begin conversing with Him—on *purpose*?

Don't stop reading now. We're just getting started.

CHAPTER 3

MY SHEEP HEAR MY VOICE

My sheep hear My voice, and I know them, and they follow Me; and I give eternal life to them, and they will never perish; and no one will snatch them out of My hand. My Father, who has given them to Me, is greater than all; and no one is able to snatch them out of the Father's hand. I and the Father are one (John 10:27-30 NASB).

How It All Began

It was late in 1981 and we didn't know what we were getting into. We were brand-new parents; our first child was less than a year old. Unbeknownst to us, things were about to change in our lives. The "fullness of time" had come, and God in Heaven was about to create a brand-new paradigm shift in our lives that I was not expecting, not prepared for, and certainly not wanting. Raised in a church that was founded in the 1800s, we had our beliefs down cold. I was a teacher in a church school and knew what and who was right and what was wrong. I could spot false doctrine a mile away!

We decided to attend a *safe* Campus Crusade for Christ Bible study that we thought would not threaten our doctrinal beliefs too much. After all, the local church headquarters had approved one of my friends, who was studying to be a pastor, to intern with the Campus Crusade for Christ program. *It should be safe*, I thought. So with our baby girl and playpen in tow, my wife, Derene, and I went to our first meeting—the meeting that changed everything.

I Already Knew the Answers. What Questions Could Remain?

Since it was our first meeting, I went to it expecting to have answers and not questions. Nevertheless, I was on my guard. This was not considered "normal" for anyone in our group to go outside the denomination for a Bible study. But, I was already an ordained elder in my own church at the youthful age of 26, and I knew a lot—or so I thought.

God's requirements were all-important to me and I was *into* it. I was happy with all that I was supposed to do and believe. One might even say I loved the doctrine in which I was raised. I was baptized in my church at the age of 10 and, looking back, I believe I came into a real acceptance of Christ, at least what I was able to understand about Him, in my conservative denomination.

Secrets Only I Knew

Now please understand that my secret thought-life was a mess. I struggled with all sorts of temptations, but they were *my* secrets and no one knew what I held in my heart. Nevertheless, the church members around me saw me as one who loved (at least the goal of keeping perfectly) God's holy Law. But one thing I held as a certainty one thing my doctrine decreed was this: I could not, in those years, be certain of my salvation, because it all depended, frankly, on how *well* one kept God's law.

I was doing just fine at keeping *some* of the laws. But with others, I was not doing so well. Still, I knew one had to start somewhere, and I was working on keeping the Law as best I could.

As Loren, the leader of our Bible study, took us through the Book of Romans, a book we would continue to study for a year or more, a small argument ensued about the "salvation issue." Because of my strong stance, I breathed a prayer to God that He would show me just one of the many Scriptures I'd known for years. I wanted to demonstrate from Scripture that it's what we *do* and how we *obey* that matters to God—not some "assurance of salvation" thing. It was about showing God by our actions. The best we could ever say, I had been taught, was, "I hope I'll be 'ready' when Jesus returns."

The Power of Satan Seemed Huge

In my mind, satan was more powerful than God. At least that's how I perceived it. God had made the way through Christ for salvation—the cross was real, the cross was required—but satan was the master deceiver and, to me and everyone I was raised with, it seemed far easier to be lost than saved.

How could I elevate satan so high? It was easy, partly because Jesus had said that wide was the way to destruction and narrow the way to life. (See Matthew 7:13.) Even Jesus, I reasoned, had taught us that it was easier to be lost than to be saved, at least in my way of thinking.

I Was Going to Prove Him Wrong

So at this Campus Crusade Bible study, I borrowed a Bible so I could speak truth to this group of about 12 people. As I furiously searched for even one clue to prove I was right about the salvation issue, my mind could not recall a single Scripture that proved my point. Instead, the Bible fell open to a Scripture that I had never seen, though I was a licensed Church School Teacher for my denomination. Truly, I had *never* seen this Scripture in my life. Suddenly, it was as if everything went into slow motion. It felt like what people have described about what happens to them in the middle of an auto accident—everything slowed way down. I was in slow motion as I read this Scripture to myself. I remember my face flushing red as I took it in. I read it over and over again to myself:

*My sheep hear **My voice**, and I know them, and they follow Me; and **I give eternal life to them, and they shall never perish;***

and no one shall snatch them out of My hand. My Father, who has given them to Me, is greater than all; and no one is able to snatch them out of the Father's hand. I and the Father are one (John 10:27-30 NASB, emphasis added).

I sat in stunned silence. So awesome was this revelation to me personally at that moment that I continued to read those verses over and over, while the conversation continued on around me. Somehow I knew my life had just changed forever; but at the moment, only God and I knew it.

A Sudden Paradigm Shift

In one verse—*one verse*—God had instantly and forever changed the three most important paradigms of my life. First, God talks to His sheep; second, we can hear His voice; and third, my salvation was certain! I pondered about hearing His voice and trusting Him with our lives—He promised. He promised that satan could not snatch me—or anyone—out of His hand once we were *in* His hand.

I simply couldn't believe it!

Toward the end of the meeting, I could hold my peace no longer. I opened up to my friends there, all of whom were from my same denomination, so they believed as I did, except for the leader and his wife and one other couple.

I blurted out, "You guys aren't going to believe this Scripture. I've never seen this before. I was just trying to disprove what was being said here, and I stumbled onto this. How come I've never seen this Scripture before?" I read it out loud to the group.

I don't remember much after that. It's still a blur. But, soon, we all knelt to pray, as we did each evening. I would later discover that our friend, Claudia, had become so shocked and yet so overjoyed and full of praise to God at this *new* revelation (she'd never seen that Scripture before either), that she silently had a profound, unprecedented experience with the Lord. It would be six months before she had the courage to tell us about it. More about that later.

In those years, Campus Crusade for Christ, a fairly conservative organization, was not exactly promoting supernatural experiences. Nevertheless, Loren had no idea of the dramatic changes he had helped to launch in our lives through his simple obedience in that evening Bible study. Not only was our understanding of Scripture being dramatically and instantly changed, but also our understanding of the supernatural had been sparked, even though it was not Loren's intention to do so.

Introduction to the Holy Spirit

You can't see Him, but He *is* a person. His name is the Holy Spirit. And He was up to something. I never heard a voice that night—or so I thought. No angel grabbed me by the arm. I didn't have a strong impression to turn to some Scripture. I just "stumbled" (if you believe it was actually a stumble) upon an unknown passage, and the Spirit of God had lifted it—in almost 3D, slow motion—off the page to change my life forever! It was time, in God's time clock, for Steve Shultz to finally get a clue, smell the coffee, wake up, and understand that God talks to me. It was time for me, accompanied by my wife, Derene, to begin the journey of learning to hear God speak, while at the same time learning that He could be trusted with our lives and even fixing our present and future mistakes. This might seem simple to some of you, but this was *revolutionary* for Derene and me.

God was telling me in that kairos moment that He was going to teach me—as the old song goes—that *"He walks with me, and He talks with me, and **He tells me** I am His own. And the joy WE share, as we tarry there, none other has ever known."* The old hymnwriters knew something that had been lost through the years. The song continues, ***"He speaks, and the sound of His voice*** *is so sweet the birds hush their singing, And the melody that He gave to me* *within my heart is ringing..."* (Taken from "In the Garden" by C. Austin Miles.)

What Was Not Real, Became Real

I'd sung that old song all my life, but up to that moment, it hadn't been real to me. It would be years before I would equate some of those old hymns with the fact that the writers and composers were in touch with the voice of God—even back then. This truth can be found everywhere in those old hymns. The writer of that old song had to have understood that God *really* walks and talks with His people! To me, the words of the hymn had been music on the piano and words on a page. They were never real in my life. Now they are.

As I write this, many years have passed; and it is important for me to teach others through this book some of what God has taught me on this journey. It's time for you, and anyone you give this book to, to learn that He not only talks—but *He has been talking* to you all along. Even when you didn't know it was His voice you were hearing. What's more, many of you who are reading this page are certain you've never heard God speak to you—"not even once," you would say. And yet, you've obeyed His voice over and over and over again. And you pleased God by doing so.

You see, God cannot lie. You are His sheep, if you have received Christ into your life. Jesus said, *"My sheep hear My voice."* I'm sorry if you feel you haven't heard Him speak. Here's a little hint, by the way. Jesus said this:

> *Jesus answered, "No one can come to Me unless the Father who sent Me draws him, and I will raise him up at the last day. It is written in the Prophets:* **'They will all be taught by God.'** **Everyone who listens to the Father and learns from Him comes to Me"** (John 6:43-45).

News Flash! According to holy Scripture (re-read the above verse if you have to), you could not have come to Jesus unless you had first listened to the Father and learned from Him, as He was teaching you.

Let me say it again another way: You would not be serving Christ today had you not listened specifically to the Father's voice when He taught you and showed you how to follow Jesus. Welcome to the club of those who hear the voice of God. By the way, every believer is in the same club—or should we call it school—the school of the Spirit. You've already been initiated.

Now that's just plain *good news*!

CHAPTER 4
TODAY WHEN YOU HEAR HIS VOICE...

*Today, **(when) you hear His voice,** do not harden your hearts as in the rebellion* (Hebrews 3:15 ESV, emphasis added).

I'm always asking my wife, "What day is it today?" Maybe it's my busy schedule or just my disorganization, but I rarely remember what day it is. When I ask, "What day is it today?" whether the answer is Tuesday, Thursday, or another day of the week—the answer is actually always the same. As corny as it sounds, according to the Word, the real answer is, *"Today is **today!**"*

Now, many versions of the Bible translate Hebrews 3:15 as, "Today, *IF* you hear His voice, do not harden your hearts as they did in the rebellion." But, as I studied this Scripture, the context of this passage intrigued me. The writer of Hebrews keeps repeating himself as he quotes the Holy Spirit about that one word: *today*. The context implies every single day. And I wondered if the word *when* might be a better translation. So, I called my Hebrew-speaking, good friend, Yehuda, and asked him how a rabbi would translate this Scripture. You see, in the original language, one of the translated definitions of the word used in this passage is *"when."*

Let me be clear. God is saying, in context, in the New Testament, that *when* you hear God's voice today, don't harden your heart. Most people, the vast majority I think, believe that God doesn't talk to *them*, if He talks to *anyone at all*. But the reality is, He not only talks to some, He talks to everyone—and He does it every single day! Like *today*, for instance.

TODAY, WHEN YOU HEAR HIS VOICE...
God's Voice Is a Call to Action!

When we were kids, my mother used to say, when her six children were misbehaving, "I'm not talking to hear myself think!" Neither is God. When He speaks to you every day, He has a purpose. God wants to tell you to change something or encourage you, to change or encourage your friends, to change the Church, or to change the world. He may only ask you to pray about what you hear, or He may ask you to go tell someone what He said so they will be edified.

Learn to Hear God's Voice—Hearing With Purpose

I'll jump ahead in my story to 1994, when I flew to Indiana to take an advanced course in learning to hear God's voice. The course quickly began to bear some very interesting fruit. God was about to use me to encourage some people—during the "today" referred to in Hebrews.

By the way, did you know that Jesus had to learn to hear and obey God? Shocking, but true. Check this out: *"Although He [Jesus] was a son,* **He learned obedience** *from what He suffered..."* (Hebrews 5:8, emphasis added).

I spent about four days in Indiana learning to hear His voice better. The final instructions given to the group were that we should keep using and practicing the gift of hearing God's voice and telling others what we were hearing. The reason is that the same Book of Hebrews says, *"But solid food is for the mature,* **who by constant use** *have* **trained themselves** *to distinguish good from evil"* (Hebrews 5:14, emphasis added).

God talks to us daily to help us to know good from evil in our lives and the lives of others. Knowing what to do, what decisions to make, what to avoid—is another way of saying that we know good from evil. Jesus said the Holy Spirit was sent to lead us into "all truth." (See John 16:13.) So, how does He lead? The fact is that most people have never heard the audible voice of

God and yet, somehow, the Holy Spirit leads us. How, then, does the Holy Spirit lead us?

He, the Holy Spirit, speaks in our language, often into our thoughts; so, we actually hear God speak even when we don't realize we're hearing Him. Through practice, you can learn from the Lord to discern right and wrong, good and evil, *by constant use of the gifts of God*. You begin to learn to distinguish which are *your* thoughts and which are *God's* thoughts.

And sometimes, to be honest, we don't know where a given thought comes from—ourselves or God.

Practice Increases the Gift

During that Indiana training I went through, which was about to pay off, I was taught that even Timothy had to be reminded to stir up the gift that had been given to him by the laying on of hands: "*Therefore* [Timothy] *I remind you to stir up the gift of God which is in you through the laying on of my hands*" (2 Timothy 1:6 NKJV). There was an obedience factor for Timothy to pay attention to. He had to choose to stir up the gift that was *already* within him.

I returned from my prophetic training back to my home church. At the very next church service, those who needed prayer for anything (especially if they were sick), were invited to come over to the side of the building for prayer. This was a common practice in our church. My chance had come; it was my time to practice the gift that is in all of us, the gift of hearing God's voice.

When We Pray, God Often *Answers*—He *Speaks*

One young woman, who was visiting our church that day, was the only one who didn't have someone praying for her when I approached the group asking for prayer. She was dressed very conservatively, had a serious look, and certainly did not seem like one who was ready to join a sports team. I asked her what the problem was. She told me her wrist hurt and said she'd been having ongoing problems with it. I asked if I could hold her wrist and pray for it, and she said that was fine. But I was now trained to listen and watch more carefully about what else God might want to say to her.

As I prayed for her wrist, suddenly a picture popped into my head. It was a picture of her singing in front of kids, even doing camp songs. From there, the picture and impression enlarged, just as I'd been practicing in Indiana. I said, "I *hear* the Lord saying that you are—or will be—working with young kids and youth." Immediately she began to cry, tears streaming down her face. I'm sure I said a few more things, but I no longer remember them, though I do remember that I asked her if that "word" meant anything to her.

"Yes, it means everything to me," she said. "I have been the youth leader at my own church for several years. But I've just been removed from that position." She didn't explain why, but watching the tears flow down her face, I could see that it had caused her great pain. She went on to explain how she was a volleyball coach, or something to that effect. She was, in fact, everything she did not *appear* to be on the outside—an outgoing, athletic, leader of youth.

Before leaving, I encouraged her by telling her that the Lord would not have revealed this word to me unless He had a desire to encourage her and bring her back into the type of ministry she loved, but perhaps with another church. I don't know who went home more encouraged. Her? Or me?

Taking It to the Streets

I was curious to see if this would work on the street. Of course I knew it would, but I'd never intentionally tried it. By accident, yes, but never on purpose. Pure fear—that's what I was facing. A few weeks later, I would have my answer. We had gone down to California on a family vacation. I was eager to get home and we were just a few hours away. We stopped in Medford, Oregon, to get a bite of dinner before we began the last leg of our journey. There, in this family restaurant, we ordered our meal and began the normal wait for our food. My eye caught a small, elderly woman a few tables up and in the next row of booths. My eyes were drawn to her.

"Why am I drawn to this woman?" I asked myself. I had a sense of what the answer was, but would I *harden* my heart to it? Would I harden my heart to God's encouraging word for this woman? I did not tell my wife or my family what I was thinking about doing. I realized that God did, in fact, want to speak to this woman to encourage her. But what did He want to say? I spent most of the meal listening on purpose to what the Lord had for her. Still, I said nothing about it to anyone.

Making a Deal With God

I made a deal with the Lord. "Lord, if she gets up and walks out the door before we finish, I will go outside that door and speak the word I believe You're telling me." You might say it was a "chicken" deal with the God of the universe. The restaurant was quiet and I didn't want to embarrass her, nor did I want to be embarrassed. So I ate fast and waited and watched. She paid her bill and walked out the door. "I have to go talk to that woman," I told Derene. "I think I'm supposed to give her a word from the Lord." To fulfill my part of the bargain, I followed her right out the door. "Excuse me," I said. She stopped and turned around, puzzled. "You don't know me," I said, "and this may seem a little strange, but when you were in the restaurant, the Lord began to talk to me about you. I wanted to tell you what He said."

She seemed confused—but she stopped and listened. I continued, "The Lord said He's seen your tears and your loneliness and He's going to bring help for you. I even *saw* someone in the military coming to you."

She started to cry. "What is this?" she asked. "I've never

heard of anything like this before," she said with tears in her eyes.

"Does that mean anything to you?" I asked.

"Yes, it does. Three weeks ago, I buried my husband. We always came to this restaurant—every week *on this day*. I'm so lonely. And I have a son who is in the military," she continued.

"Well, I just wanted you to know that God sees you and knows about your loneliness, and He wanted me to encourage you and let you know that help is on the way."

She was nearly speechless and didn't know how to respond. She told me that she was a Christian and that she had prayed a lot to God lately. I ended the conversation with, "Well, God just wants you to know that He's watching out for you and He hasn't forgotten about you. I'll see you later."

"Goodbye," she said in a thankful voice, and that was that.

Don't Harden Your Heart

There have been many times when I too have hardened my heart when God spoke to me. Sometimes I have the strongest impression to do something. But then I talk myself out of it.

Sound familiar?

We've all experienced it. I'm not talking about the guilt feelings we all have—those feelings that make us feel that we should do more for the Lord. Not at all!

I'm talking about those impressions you have that suggest that you should talk to a certain person, make a phone call to a particular woman, or simply tell someone at church that you're praying for them. Maybe you've even just had the thought that you should smile at the cashier and tell him or her, "Looks like you're having a hard day. This must be a tough job. I'll pray for you tonight." (Don't forget to pray.)

God puts those thoughts into our minds all the time. It's His voice, but it's very easy to harden your heart because of fear. This Scripture in Hebrews 3:15 is about trusting God: *"Today, if you hear His voice," for everything*—for what God will do *for* you, for what God will do *to* you, and for what God will do *through* you.

You can trust God in this—His voice, I mean. I know I'm being repetitive, but this is important. Repetition is the mother of learning and most of us do not get the message the first time. God talks to you **all the time**. So, *"Today,* **when** *you hear His voice, do not harden your hearts…"* (Hebrews 3:15 ESV).

What I didn't realize when my journey began is how many *whens* during my *todays* were ahead of me. It's a good thing, because I wouldn't have believed it. There's a fear factor in learning to hear God's voice. The fear is that God Himself will give you special assignments or you fear you may get it wrong. It may help if I share more of my own prophetic assignments with you.

God Often Speaks in Riddles?

What do you mean God often speaks in riddles? He is supposed to talk clearly, isn't He?

Personally, I'd love it if God spoke plainly, in my language—without riddles—every single time. But He doesn't. That is something I have learned to accept and deal with.

What do I mean? Didn't God say He now speaks plainly? Let me ask you a question. When it was all over—after Christ had died on the Cross, and after the Resurrection had taken place—and at the end of the preceding 40 days of Christ remaining on the earth, what did Jesus say?

"Wait here until what the Father has promised comes to you…

you shall receive power..." (Acts 1:4, 8, author's paraphrase).

When Jesus ascended, His followers were told by an angel, *"Why stand here gazing up? He'll be back in the same way. Go back and do as He told you"* (Acts 1:11, author's paraphrase). Now, in my book, that indicates that they did not plainly understand all things. They had the world's Creator right there in their midst for three and a half years, plus they witnessed the Crucifixion and the Resurrection, and then another 40 days, and they still did not understand many, many things.

Why?

Because even when God speaks plainly, sometimes He has to say what He wants to say by the mouth of two or three witnesses and then He has to say these things over and over—sometimes in a dream, sometimes through the mouth of a heathen, sometimes through a vision, and sometimes in a riddle form. There are many other examples. I believe almost every person and every prophet receives most things in riddle form first, if not mostly in riddles all the time.

This is one of God's ways. Even when He speaks plainly, His words are passing through the grid of our understanding, which is often based on false paradigms, false theology, false understanding of His ways, and on and on. So when He speaks plainly, it really is PLAIN—to *Him*. But to us, we have to "work it out with fear and trembling," because not all things are clear the first time we hear them. Our minds sometimes prevent us from understanding what we are hearing. So, God has to come to us in many ways in order to get His word to us.

In fact, I often tell people: If you think you fully understand the word you are about to give and the effect it will have, think again.

CHAPTER 5

YOU CAN'T STOP GOD; HE'S ALREADY SPEAKING

"...My word that goes out from My mouth: it will not return to Me empty, but will accomplish what I desire and achieve the purpose for which I sent it" (Isaiah 55:11).

"But, will it fly, Orville?"

This is the question people humorously surmise that Wilbur must have asked his brother Orville in 1903 about their new invention America's first, heavier-than-air flying machine. It was the first contraption that was created to take off and maintain sustained flight under its own power. In those days, only a few men and women actually believed that a machine with its various heavy components, manned by one or more persons, could actually be made to fly as if lighter than air. But the truth is—from nearly the beginning of history—all that was needed to make sustained flight happen was *already* in place. This includes the law of aerodynamics, gravity, the science of headwinds, tailwinds, and the immutable law that for every action there is an equal and opposite reaction. Even wood, metal, and the ability to build a capable motor long pre-existed the birth of the Wright brothers. Yet, until Wilbur and Orville Wright took advantage of what was *already there*, no plane had taken flight above the earth. The first flight lasted just an insignificant 59 seconds, but that small step allowed a "giant leap for mankind" when, only 66 years later, Neil Armstrong would stun the world as his feet touched the moon's surface—250,000 miles away from our own planet Earth.

What prevented all of this from happening sooner? The answer is simple. Mankind had not taken advantage of what had

What Has Been There "All Along" for the Church?

It's the same with today's worldwide Church. All along God has been saying that when He speaks, things *will* happen. Not that things *might* happen, but what God says will happen. God speaks and His spoken Word never, ever fails!

Jesus said we were to ask God for our daily bread—both literal and spiritual bread, I believe. How could He give it to us if He doesn't speak it into existence every day first?

> *"... My word that goes out from My mouth: it will not return to Me empty, but will accomplish what I desire and achieve the purpose for which I sent it"* (Isaiah 55:11).

The most amazing thing about this passage is the depth of its meaning. It means if God speaks to us, we *must* hear Him, knowingly or unknowingly, because He said His word would accomplish what He desires. How could it accomplish its purpose if we do not hear that word, even if we are sure we don't hear God? Thus, since we *do* hear God speak when we are not even trying to—then how much more will we be able to hear Him if we do try to hear Him? He told us we would find Him if we searched for Him with all our heart. This includes our thought process, by the way. *"And you will seek Me and find Me when you search for Me with all your heart"* (Jeremiah 29:13 NASB).

God has declared His voice to us—as an established fact—in a multitude of ways. Here are just a few of them, paraphrased:

- "My sheep hear (or listen to) My voice" (John 10:27).

- "Everyone who listens to the Father will come to Him." (See John 6:43-46.)

- "My word will not return to Me empty but will accomplish what I desire" (Isaiah 55:11).

- "In the last days, My Spirit will fall upon men and women, young and old, male and female, for dreams, visions, and prophesying (listening to His voice and telling others what He says)" (Joel 2 and Acts 2).

- "If anyone lacks wisdom, let him ask God for it, who gives it liberally," as God talks to give that wisdom (James 1:5).

- "Call to Me and I will answer and *show* you things you don't know of" (Jeremiah 33:3).

- "Your ears will hear a voice behind you telling you which way to turn" (Isaiah 30:21).

God's kind intentions toward you are: *"Whether you turn to the right or to the left, your ears will hear a voice behind you, saying, 'This is the way; walk in it'"* (Isaiah 30:21).

Some people call that "spooky" or "strange." God calls it grace and a fulfilled promise.

All May Hear His Voice

The Scripture is simply chock-full of references assuring us that God will speak personally to us—in one way or another—in both the Old and New Testament. Believers in every Christian denomination—all along—have both taught their people and *believed themselves* that God's people can—and *do*—hear the voice of God. Not just a select few, but all of us! Now that's a gutsy claim. I challenge you to examine old and popular hymns to prove what I am saying.

"Prove it!" you may demand.

Ask yourself if you've ever used a phrase similar to one or

more of these:

- "I just felt impressed to go a different way home, and I was there just in time to help someone who really needed me."

- "I prayed about that bad situation, and then I suddenly felt a real peace that God had answered my prayer."

- "What a coincidence! I ran into that person just when I needed his advice."

- "I asked God for a job and then later the thought came to me about calling this one man, and he hired me on the spot."

- "I feel like God intervened in my situation and it came to me just what to tell that person who was upset. I feel like God showed me just what to say. Thank You, God!"

- "For some reason, I decided to leave a few minutes earlier than normal and just missed that huge traffic jam."

- "That's strange. I dreamed about that very thing last night!"

- "I don't know how, but I knew the answer to that and I hadn't even studied it."

- "That was a 'divine appointment' if I've ever seen one. I was really able to encourage Joe when he was so discouraged and I didn't even know I'd see him today."

- "Just when I decided to call my mother, I found out she desperately needed to talk to me. She was so discouraged."

- "As I read my Bible, that Scripture just sort of jumped

off the page at me. I've been thinking about it all day."

- "I don't know why people always pour their life story out to me, but I seem to have just the counsel they need, when they need it. I don't know why that is."

- "I've sung, 'What A Friend We Have In Jesus' for years. What if it's true?"

If you've made any of these comments, then by your words, you are acknowledging that you do hear God's voice speaking to you, even if you insist you've never heard Him speak. And you've taught or modeled the same.

Listening to His Voice—My Journey Continued

Back to 1982. Over a year had passed with our new Bible study group, the one where God had showed me that He speaks and that I was safe in Him. Through this intervention by God in my life, I'd developed an insatiable and surprising desire for His Word—more than I had ever known in my life. It was the kind of desire for Scripture that I'd only envied as I'd heard others speak about it.

With this new passion, I would often sit in front of the TV (as was my normal habit), but now, the TV was only background noise, because my Bible was always in my lap and I would pore over it night after night. The odd thing was, it mattered not if I was reading the Old or New Testaments, all I saw was *grace—the Gospel of Grace*! Something had awakened within me in the last year and I would never be the same. I was apprehended by God's love!

That which had appeared stale and hard to understand in Scripture form, was now almost jumping off the page as I read the Bible. I would only later understand that when God's written Word comes alive like this, it is *no less* the voice of God than it is when we hear His voice audibly.

Jesus Himself said, *"No one can come to Me unless the Father who sent Me draws him..."* (John 6:44). I was being drawn, as He bid me to come closer. He was using His voice of course. Even the Holy Spirit speaks! *How is he going to draw you unless he speaks to you.*

This wasn't some strange "force," like what we see in "Star Wars," that had me glued to my Bible while in front of the television set. It was the Father's voice. He was speaking to me—not in words that I could hear and understand and repeat. But somehow, He was causing the words to come alive. I can now imagine that He was actually saying things such as, "Look at that Scripture. See how My grace is all over that?" I would turn to my wife and read passages to her. "Look at all this grace!" I would say over and over again. "How could I never have seen this before?"

God was now ready to take us to the next level—the level of actually responding to His Word as it jumped off the page.

Thanksgiving Miracle

Claudia had been with us in the Campus Crusade Bible study that first night and had experienced perhaps the greatest joy of all of us when she heard me read the Scripture from John chapter 10 out loud. Remember the Scripture? *"My sheep listen to My voice; I know them, and they follow Me. I give them eternal life, and they shall never perish; no one can snatch them out of My hand"* (John 10:27-28).

Now, roughly a year later, Claudia complained of her chronic and major health problem. She had severe arthritis and it was causing her increasingly awful pain. I worked with her at an office in town and noticed that her tennis shoes were thin and old for a reason—so that her swollen arthritis could poke through the holes. Her hands were visibly arthritic. We would often eat dinner, cafeteria-style, at Claudia and Patrick's house. As she dished food out to each person, she would have to hold each plate with two hands because the pain caused by supporting a plate of food with only one hand was unbearable. She was not even 30 years old, yet her pain didn't match her age.

One night at the Bible study Claudia cried out, "I'm not asking God to heal me." Of course, at that time, she didn't exactly believe that God would or could heal people. "I'm only asking that He make the pain less severe, so I can do what I need to do as a mother." The leader, Loren, was finding himself in new places with the Lord as well. Campus Crusade for Christ wasn't exactly encouraging their people to teach about praying for healing of bodies. However, from somewhere, having heard God speak in his heart (though I'm sure he did not hear Him speak in audible words), Loren found the faith to say, "Well, the Bible does say that if anyone is sick, he should call for the elders to pray for them."(See James 5:14.) *"Why don't we pray for you, Claudia, the next time we get together?"*

Obeying God's Voice in Scripture

Now, take special note. Many say that the "canon of Scripture" is all there is and God isn't doing anything beyond that Word. They seem to think that since we have the Scriptures, we don't need a personal word from God. That sounds very holy, of course, but the canon of Scripture says we should pray for the sick. Now, on the one hand, we weren't exactly the elders of the church. On the other hand, Loren was the leader of this particular tiny home group and we were "two or more" gathering together in Jesus' name. Did that make us "elders" though? Then you have Jesus saying we would do the same things He did — and even more: *"I tell you the truth, anyone who has faith in Me will do what I have been doing. He will do even* **greater things than** *these, because I am going to the Father"* (John 14:12, emphasis added).

Stretching What Little Faith We Had

As suggested, the next week we got together for Bible study and prayer. We had a normal Bible study. Then we all gathered around the coffee table in front of the couch to pray for Claudia. Someone got some Wesson cooking oil from the cupboard. (What? Not even olive oil from the Middle East?) We knelt down.

It seemed like we should kneel for something like this, right? As we put some oil on Claudia, not knowing how it should be done, we prayed perhaps the weakest, faith-absent prayers you have ever heard being prayed.

You'll recognize one of our phrases: "Lord, heal her *if* it be Your will, and it's OK; if it's not, would You at least help Claudia's arthritis to be better?"

One at a time, around the table we prayed. Our prayers were so dry! I didn't feel an ounce of faith in the room. Maybe someone there might have had more than me, though, who knows? It sure didn't feel like anyone had an ounce of faith, however. After nearly ten minutes of this kind of praying, we stopped. We had all prayed everything we could think of to pray. I distinctly remember people clearing their throats and making excuses to get up to go to the restroom or whatever—just some excuse to end this seeming charade.

No one was brave enough to ask Claudia about her condition. We didn't want to put her—or us, on the spot. Embarrassed, we disbursed and Claudia went into the master bedroom.

Suddenly, back in the bedroom, Claudia stumbled back and had to catch herself as she almost fell down. Some sort of power was on her, or hit her, or made her feel weak or something. It lasted just a moment. A few minutes later she came out of the room and her eyes met Derene's eyes, as they met in the hallway.

Somewhere deep within Derene, from a place she had never known before, something inside her suddenly *knew*—it was clear to her as she looked at Claudia. "Claudia, you're healed, aren't you?" Derene said excitedly.

"I don't understand it, Derene," Claudia said, dazed, as she told her about almost falling down when this power hit her. "I don't feel any pain anywhere!" She began to bend and twist her back, open and close her hands, and feel her feet. The pain was gone!

What Happens When You Obey

We had obeyed the "voice of God" through *both* the written Word and Loren's impression from the Lord to finally do something instead of just talking about it. That's how you start hearing the voice of God, by the way. Do what the Word says. God often won't give you more until you do what He's already told you to do. Suddenly that mustard-seed faith had resulted in Claudia being healed of arthritis!

"But is she *still* healed?" you might be asking. Yes! Many years later she is still arthritis-free! Within two weeks of that prayer, all evidence of swelling was gone, the pain was gone, and now she wears brand-new tennis shoes to show off! To this day Claudia is arthritis-free.

Being Led Into All Truth

Jesus told His friends that He needed to go away because: *"...I am telling you nothing but the truth when I say it is profitable* (good, expedient, advantageous) *for you that I go away. Because if I do not go away, the Comforter* (Counselor, Helper, Advocate, Intercessor, Strengthener, Standby) *will not come to you [into close fellowship with you]; but if I go away, I will send Him to you [to be in close fellowship with you]"* (John 16:7 AMP, emphasis added).

The Holy Spirit speaks. Jesus speaks. And the Father speaks. We call all of their speaking the voice of God! Now about the Holy Spirit, some people think that the Holy Spirit is some kind of a gaseous force, making people feel good or giving them a sense of general comfort. But the Word of God says that He, the Holy Spirit, is a Person who speaks:

"While they were worshiping the Lord and fasting, the Holy Spirit ***said,*** *'Set apart for Me Barnabas and Saul for the work to which I have called them.' So after they had fasted and prayed, they placed their*

hands on them and sent them off." (Acts 13:2-3, emphasis added).

When you pray, the Holy Spirit doesn't just warm you up or cool you down, though sometimes you feel only that. He speaks to you—as He spoke to Loren. And as He spoke to Claudia, telling her to bring up the subject of her arthritis. Neither Claudia nor Loren heard an audible voice in their heads, but both responded to the voice that they *didn't hear*. That's how it begins for many people. And that's how it will likely begin with you!

Those Safe "Impressions"

Before I was willing to admit that I believed God could or would talk to me, I readily spoke in terms of what I felt "impressed" by God to do, in the same way Loren felt "impressed" to obey the written Word where others might have said, "Oh, that doesn't apply today—in our time."

Do you want to begin to hear God speak? Seriously? Then I have an assignment for you. Sometimes I do mini-seminars on learning to hear the voice of God. I can boil an all-day course on learning to hear God's voice into just three simple words. And here they are: *"Follow your impressions!"*

We are often spellbound by the stories of others who have been impressed by God to do things—and then they ended up with phenomenal, miraculous "divine appointments," or divine encounters or unexplained "coincidental happenings," which have the stamp of God on them. When they tell those stories, rarely does their storytelling include details of an angel from Heaven grabbing their arm and pulling them "just in time" to their perfectly choreographed assignment by God, though sometimes this can occur.

That's not how it normally works. Normally, if God or an angel speaks or acts, you are hardly aware of it. But you can practice becoming aware.

The only explanation for these appointments by God is that those involved in these appointments had *heard God's voice*—whether they knew it or not—and usually in these stories, they didn't know it was God's voice until after the story was over.

Like It or Not...

If you've ever told anyone you had one of those *coincidental* divine encounters, then you've heard God's voice and you've obeyed it. Let me repeat it again, so I can hammer the point home: you have already heard God's voice, even if you've never heard it audibly. Since you became a Christian, you've heard His voice! Actually, before anyone was saved they heard God speaking!

But *how* you hear His voice—through your own filters—now that's a different story altogether.

CHAPTER 6
DIVINE APPOINTMENTS—A WAY TO LISTEN TO GOD

This may come as a shock to you, but the Earth—the round sphere we call our planet—has no ears. Now, that's just a silly thing to say, isn't it? And yet, when God spoke, the Earth—without ears—heard, responded, obeyed, or whatever you choose to call it.

> *"...And the **Spirit of God** moved upon the face of the waters. **And God said**, Let there be light: and there was light. And God saw the light, that it was good: and God divided the light from the darkness"* (Genesis 1:2-4 KJV, emphasis added).

Why make such a silly point? The answer is simple. God speaks, and whatever and whoever He speaks to, responds to His voice.

> *"So is My Word that goes out from My mouth: It will not return to Me empty, **but will accomplish** what I desire and achieve the purpose for which I sent it"* (Isaiah 55:11, emphasis added).

Divine Appointments—the Result of the Voice of God

When I was a teenager, our family went on vacation. We were riding in one of the first motor homes manufactured. That's how my dad was. He had to have the first of many things. When no one had motor homes, we bought a motor home that cost as much as a house in 1962.

When video tape recorders became available, Dad had one of the first. In the 1960s people were shocked that he could aim a camera and moments later, he could rewind the black-and-white, reel-to-reel tape, and play back what had just been videotaped.

One day while on vacation, as we drove in our motor home on the California freeway, we had forgotten to push in the step that was on the side of the motor home. This was a driving hazard, and it was certainly not legal. Soon a highway patrolman's red light was flashing and we pulled over. "I've stopped you because your step is out," he told us, as we all began to see smoke seeping out of the engine. Opening the engine compartment, accessible only from within the motor home, flames burst forth, as fresh oxygen from the opening fueled the fire. The entire motor was on fire! Dad reached for his fire extinguisher, but it wasn't enough to extinguish it. The fire blazed. The highway patrolman ran to his car and grabbed his own fire extinguisher—it was just enough to put out the fire!

Coincidence? Forget about using that word. God is in control of the affairs of man. He had spoken into the destiny of this family of eight people, determining that we would not suddenly perish inside that motor home that day with an engine that could have easily exploded. Certainly, He could have prevented the fire in the first place. But, you see, God is a relational God and He is constantly at work, showing Himself to be faithful.

Only Heaven knows at what moment in time God spoke. Did He speak and we left the step out? Did He speak and the highway patrolman noticed it at that exact moment, though we had been driving for hours? Did He speak when my dad bought the fire extinguisher weeks earlier? Did He speak when the patrolman had been told earlier in the year to begin to carry a fire extinguisher? Truly, only God knows. And no one went home that night having reported how well that they had heard God speak.

But God had spoken and light came into darkness—and that light was "very good."Our family had a divine appointment with the policeman and that appointment saved our lives. We simply don't know just how many appointments we have had in our lifetimes that have saved our lives.

This applies to every one of us.

Divine Appointments — A Way God Loves to Talk

Let me be honest with you. I *love* the subject of divine appointments. I think that's because this is the most misunderstood way that *God speaks loudly* into your life and mine.

Who do you know that doesn't have an amazing story of how God seemed to intervene in a most unusual way in their life — just when they most needed it? And yet rarely does that story include anyone hearing an audible voice, or even an impression in one's mind.

Most of these stories are so out of "left field!"

You didn't hear a voice. You didn't feel an angel grab you by the arm. And yet, at the right time and at just the right place, in a perfect way, *God came through for you*, while remaining virtually silent and anonymous. Am I right?

When it happens to me, and it happens to me *a lot*, I'm always left asking, **"How did He do that? How in the world did God do that?"**

How Did He Do That?

The thing about God is that He is a talking, communicating, relational God. That's the way *He is*. He's never *not* the way He is as odd as that sounds to say.

That is why He clarifies in John 10:27-30, *"My sheep listen to* [they hear] *My voice; I know them, and they follow Me. I give them eternal life, and they shall never perish; no one will snatch them out of*

My hand. My Father, who has given them to Me, is greater than all; no one can snatch them out of My Father's hand. I and the Father are one."

Without trying to, without intending to, without struggling to, God's sheep—that's you and me—both listen to and *hear* the *Lord's voice.* It's inevitable!

Let me say it again another way: "You *can't not* hear God's voice!"

It's something believers just do. Even when you're sure you don't do it—*you do it!* You *hear* God's voice.

It's impossible to *not* hear. It's in the spiritual atmosphere of the very air you and I breathe; within that atmosphere is the *voice of God,* always speaking, always blessing, always protecting His sheep.

We hear *Him,* try or not. We *hear Him. You* hear Him.

That is how divine appointments are even possible at all! The way you ended up at the right place at the right time is that you had hundreds of impressions to turn this way, or stop and wait, or hesitate, or rush, and on and on. Then at just the right time you end up right where God wants you—*at the exact time He wants you there!*

Planes, Trains, and Automobiles with God

Just like you, most of my divine appointments (AKA divine encounters or divine interventions) occur outside of my own home, and mostly, since I travel a lot, they happen outside of my own town and even my own state.

This is as it was meant to be. This is why Jesus said we were to go out into the highways and byways of life, to *compel them to come in!*

What are the highways and byways? Trains, planes, and automobiles of course. And airports, gas stations, banks, malls, and at church.

So, as I mention in another chapter, we are often exhorted by Holy Spirit to go out onto the highways of life and "go compelling" today. Have *you* gone compelling lately? That is when we offer our lives so publically for *Him*, in front of those who don't know Him, that we present a *most compelling* picture of the Savior. And they feel *compelled* to come into the Kingdom of God—to possess that very Person whom we possess.

"I Want That Seat Up There," I Said...Or Was That Me at All?

It was the day after the San Francisco earthquake of 1989. I was only just beginning to understand that God was walking and talking with me—*all the time!*

During the earthquake there was that large bridge in San Francisco Bay that lost a huge section. Literally, a portion of the bridge fell into the Bay. One car nearly went off the bridge (while others had already gone off). The man who almost went off had one of those early cell phones. Few people had them in those days. He was able to call for help. Keep this fact in mind, as it plays into this story.

So, the next morning, with the knowledge of earthquakes strongly in the news, I boarded my plane from my home city—Dallas, Texas.

These were the days when planes had many empty seats on each flight, a luxury virtually non-existent today. After the plane was well into the air and the seatbelt light went off, I looked up ahead at a seat I was eyeing. It was an aisle seat with an empty seat in the middle.

"Yes," I said to myself, "I'm going to get that seat—an aisle seat with an empty middle seat!"

I moved quickly to my newfound location, and after a time I struck up a conversation with the older woman in the window seat. Soon, we were talking about the San Francisco earthquake that happened the day before.

She went on to tell me it was *her son* who was in the car that didn't quite go off the bridge. He had used his cell phone to call for help! Wow, what a coincidence!

However, I knew enough by then to know that when a coincidence is just "too coincidental," it's a sign that something else is up—something more important.

So, I began to intentionally listen more closely to what she had to say.

"Could this be a divine appointment?" I asked myself.

After a while we compared traveling notes.

"Where are you heading to?" I asked her.

"Well, when we land in Tennessee, I take another flight to Ohio."

"Ohio? Ha! I'm heading to Ohio too!" I said. "What's in Ohio?

"Well my mom had an accident the other day. She's in the hospital and I'm going to see her."

"Wow, where did this happen?"

"My flight takes me to Dayton, Ohio. From there I rent a car and drive for about an hour or so."

"Dayton? I'm going to take the same flight to Dayton!

Wow! Where is your mom in the hospital?"

"Well, there's this place called Kettering. I'm heading to Kettering Hospital where my mom is."

"You're kidding!" I almost raised my voice. "I'm heading out to Kettering too! Goodness!"

"Why are *you* going to Kettering?" She asked me.

"Well, next to Kettering Hospital is a large retirement home. It's part of the same hospital complex. I manage that retirement home from Dallas!"

"You're kidding!" She *did* raise her voice on this one. "I called that retirement home yesterday to ask if I could get a room to stay in while staying in town for my mom. They said, 'No, you can't. There's an executive flying out from Dallas who has to use our one remaining guest room.' *And you're that executive!*" she shrieked.

"I sure am!" I had to agree. "Listen, that's amazing. When we land, let me make a call and see what I can do!"

The moment we deplaned, I went to a payphone and called over, got her a room in the retirement complex, and was able to deliver the good news to her.

"You're my angel today!" she said.

Well, perhaps, in a way, I *was* her angel. But that's only because, somehow, real angels were at work pulling this whole thing together.

What Did It Look Like "Behind the Scenes"?

I would have loved to look into the *invisible* realm to watch what was going on behind the scenes. Jesus Christ, who by *His*

Spirit lives in me, was saying to me—or *in me*—"I want that seat up there. It looks more comfortable for spreading out."

So, was it *me* thinking that? Or was it the Holy Spirit speaking within me...to me...for me? And yet it wasn't *for me*—it was *for her*! He wanted to help *her*, and here I was, a willing vessel, who, as we've mentioned before, was a *sheep* who already could *hear His voice,* even when I didn't know it was His voice at all!

As it was with me, the *Lord* has many such encounters for you! And, I've discovered, the more willing the vessel (you're the vessel), the more common the supernatural intervention experiences are.

Do you *want* more experiences like this? Then simply ask Him for them and you shall have them! But record them, because God wants those stories shared and shared and shared. They are both for your benefit and of the person you meet, but beyond that, they are for the masses!

Again, *please* record your stories! Then God will give you more experiences—more divine encounters. He wants you to be telling the stories everywhere you go, for the rest of your life! His sheep need encouraging. Your stories will encourage God's sheep.

How Does God Orchestrate Encounters In a Rushing Crowd?

If you're anything like me, you sort of "get it" with God; i.e., He can take a situation where we don't see in the spirit realm, and He can manipulate your positions and those of others He wants you to meet, right? You can kind of see how He does that.

But, what if we "throw a lot at" God? What if we make it really and truly "hard" for Him—you know, like give Him no real time, not even seconds, to orchestrate an event? Why don't we just throw a situation at God where He has "no time to think" and "no place to move" and the crowd is completely chaotic?

Sounds fun, right?

Can He pull that off?

Let's just see...

Pure Chaos!

While still living in Dallas, I was on a business trip and needed to board a flight in Houston and head toward California around where I used to live in the Ontario area.

On such flights most people will find themselves flying *Southwest Airlines*. Now *Southwest* can be fun, but to board the plane...that can be pure chaos.

Why?

Because you don't get an assigned seat. No one does. If you get to the gate early enough, you might get a number from 1-30. That means you can be among the first 30 passengers to board, but when you do, it will be a mad rush for a seat—any seat at all!

You can imagine then that I normally get there early for that. I want to have great choices.

"Numbers 1 through 30 may now board!" the flight attendant called out. That means you have to rush to the gate to head into the plane, and then once in the plane, you rush up the aisle to grab a seat.

I love the aisle seat whenever I can get it. It's just me.

On this day, it was quite a rush, and everyone else ahead of me was grabbing aisle seats all the way from the front to the back. I got nearly to the back of the plane because virtually every aisle seat was gone. I don't know how I missed them, but here I was now at the very back and no aisle. I quickly turned around against the crowd and did in fact find an aisle seat where the window and middle were taken. An *odd find*, and an unusual one too! This was the last aisle seat on the entire plane.

I threw myself down on the seat and looked to my left. A nice Chinese couple sat next to me. I was so relieved to have a good seat. But I was clueless how this had even happened.

During the flight to California, I struck up a conversation with the Chinese woman next to me. She was very nice and wanted to know if I was a pastor.

"No, but why do you ask?" I inquired.

"I don't see many men in business suits reading Christian books," she said.

"Oh, well I am a Christian, but not a pastor. I'm on business."

As the flight continued, we began to compare life notes and who has been where and when. I no longer recall how we got there in conversation, but when we were finished comparing notes, this is what we discovered:

When she was five...

And when my father was also five years old...

My father and her...were playmates...

At the same kindergarten class...

At the same missionary school...

Smack dab in the middle of Mainland *China*!

Wow! Oh my goodness! Now, how did *God do that*? And more importantly...

Why did God do that?

Now my antenna was up. Clearly this was a divine encounter. When *anything* is too coincidental to be a coincidence, remember, always ask God, "What are You doing here, God?"

Later on the flight, she commented to me, "I wish my son was more like you!"

"Why do you want your son to be more like me?"

"I can see you are really a good Christian man and seeking after God. I'm so worried about my son!"

"Why are you worried about him?"

"He's going to this really strange church and I'm just worried sick. It seems like he is leaving behind everything he was taught!"

"What church is that?"

She went on to describe the church, and even gave me its specific name and location. As it turns out, I had not only been to that church myself, but I had gone there *because* it was totally a God-seeking, Holy-Spirit-honoring, Jesus-loving church. It was everything a mother would want her son to be going to.

"Listen," I said to her. I now knew why God orchestrated this divine encounter. "I've been to that church. That's an amazing God-seeking Church. If your son attends that church, then you have nothing to worry about. He goes there because he's seeking God with his whole heart!"

She was so completely happy and suddenly set at ease! And I knew that God had set this entire divine encounter up for one main thing—to help this devoted mother to stop worrying about her son!

Isn't God an amazing, *comforting*, and *thoughtful* God?

"GOD'S LIGHT IS SHINING ALL OVER YOU!" She Said

A few years after this, about 1991, we had moved back to the Great Northwest, but times were especially hard. The partners I worked for in Florida had closed the business and I was out of a job.

It was Sunday. We were helping a new startup church in Vancouver, Washington. Our faith was sky high, but our bank account was empty. By the time we'd limped back to Vancouver, I had a driver's license from Texas and plates on my car from Florida. This is illegal of course. Beyond that, our plates *were expired*!

As church was closing, we gathered into small groups to pray for one another. This one sister said she had a word for me. She said, "First, I want to tell you that I see angels! Lots and lots of angels all around you! It's just amazing to me!"

I said, "That's interesting, because Derene and I and the kids pray for angels all the time. But we never see them. It's our constant prayer!"

She continued, "This is going to sound strange, but I'm supposed to tell you this: God's light is shining all over you!"

"Wow," I said. "I wonder what that means? It sure sounds good!"

I thanked her and we headed out to take a friend of the girls' home.

Pulling in behind us was a police car, and he just stuck with us. We turned left. He turned left. We turned right. He turned right.

"Lord, help us! We have Florida plates and a Texas driver's license! That's a huge ticket IF we get stopped."

Suddenly, his red lights came on and we pulled over.

Rolling down the window, I heard the policeman say, "I see you have Florida plates, and they are expired."

"Yes, sir. We just arrived from Florida and we haven't gotten it changed over."

"Can I see your driver's license please?"

"Yes, sir. It's from Texas. We had only lived in Florida a few months after we moved there from Texas."

"Can I see your insurance card?"

"Yes, here it is—oops! Oh no! This one is expired. But I do have current insurance. I forgot to put the new card in my wallet!"

"Uh huh! I'm going to write you a citation for these things. Hold on, I'll be back in a minute with your ticket."

Our hearts sank as this was going to exceed $600 and now it was a "done deal." And where were we going to get $600?

On the way to his car, we heard his radio make a noise and he stopped and talked for a minute. He turned around and came back to our window.

I looked at him as he opened his mouth and said these exact words: "GOD'S LIGHT IS SHINING ALL OVER YOU TODAY!"

"What?" I asked.

"I just got a call. There's a fender bender around the corner that I have to get to. I'm going to let you go, but you take care of these things right away!"

"Yes, sir! And thank you so much!"

How did God do that?

How did *He* time it all? How did He know ahead of time the exact phrase for this woman to say earlier, "God's light is shining all over you today"?

What an amazing God we serve!

What a God of *grace* and *mercy* we serve!

Besides John 10:27 that you've seen in this book, *"My sheep hear My voice…and they **follow Me**,"* (NKJV, emphasis added) there is this Scripture:

> *He has shown you, O man, what is good; and what does the Lord require of you but to do justly, **to love mercy**, and to walk humbly with your God?* (Micah 6:8 NKJV, emphasis added).

God is speaking to you all the time. *All the time.* And this *God* of yours and mine, who is constantly talking to you—this God loves mercy! This God *loves kindness*!

CHAPTER 7
DOES GOD SPEAK THROUGH THE BIBLE—OR ONLY TEACH?

God has as many ways to speak as there are grains of sand on the seashore. He's creative and does things differently every time. I was recently on a flight home from a conference that we had conducted in France. There were six of us. Have you ever tried to get six seats together on a plane? It rarely works. But as my wife requested the seats, I asked for God's perfect will to be done—and I have come to learn that He answers such prayers.

The final seating was a long row of people and one seat on the aisle across the way. As long as I get an aisle seat, I'm usually happy; and after all, I was seated just across the aisle from my family. Sitting in my aisle seat, there was one man seated to my right. As often is the case (but not always), I wondered if it was God's handiwork—a divine appointment possibly—that this man was beside me. It was! Don't misunderstand me though. Most of the time, I'm content to fly in silence and read and nap.

Most of the flight I did just that: rested, read, slept, and paid no attention to anything else. But several hours prior to landing, I saw the man take out his Bible and begin to read from the Book of Joshua. *Hmm*, I thought to myself, *this could be one of those encouraging times when I'm supposed to give more hope and comfort to the believer sitting next to me.* For nearly two hours I continued to glance at him and I noticed that he was still reading. Once he opened up a card, seeming to check that he was reading the prescribed Scripture for the day.

"This is his time," I sensed the Lord saying. "He lives what he reads and he applies it to himself. "After over two hours of reading, he suddenly took out a pen and marked one short passage. I felt led to pray. *"This is his time!"* the Lord prompted me again. After a while, I got up the nerve to ask, "Are you in ministry, a pastor, or something?"

"Oh, sort of. I'm returning from a short-term missions trip to help a group in France. We go every few years."

"The reason I ask you this," I said, "is that the Lord was talking to me about you while you were reading your Bible."

He was silent.

"What passage did you underline in Joshua?" My distance eyesight is not that good, so I truly didn't know.

"Oh, just something I wanted to remember."

Stubbornness came over me. "Yes, but what specifically did you underline? I insisted. "I've watched you for almost two hours and you underlined only one section in Joshua. I just wondered what that was."

"Oh, well, I just noticed that Caleb went into the Promised Land when he was forty years old, but he was reflecting back on it in his eighties. I just hit forty myself so it made an impression on me."

"That's interesting," I said, "because I was on a ministry trip to France, too. I teach people how to listen to God for themselves. While you were reading, God told me it was *your time*. I sense He wanted you to be encouraged that this is, in fact, *your time* and many of His promises for you are about to come true."

"Well, I want to say that I strongly agree with you and I also strongly *disagree* with you!" he said, contradicting himself. He continued," I don't believe a person can take the Bible and outside of its own context, apply it to himself!"

I was amazed because he had just done that very thing. He had underlined the very part that applied to himself and now he was telling me you just can't do that—and that he disagreed with people who did such things. *That's odd*, I thought to myself. He is arguing against the very thing he's doing.

Time doesn't allow me to describe our whole conversation, but I told him I felt it was no coincidence that we were sitting together and that it was no coincidence that he had chosen *only* that one passage of Scripture to underline. I told him that God has chosen this time, this place, and this date for him—and for me—and God had chosen this man's very actions to confirm to him that it was God Himself who was speaking to Him about his life.

He said, "Well, thank you."

It was one of those, "OK, that's all I can handle right now" kind of thank yous, but it was also a true thank you, I felt. As the plane landed, his friendliness was amazing. He offered to help with my luggage and he offered for me not to let him leave the plane first, even though he was late for his connection. You see, something inside told him this was a divine encounter. I sensed he somehow knew, in his "knower," that it truly was not a coincidence, that God had spoken to him, but all his training, all his life, he'd been told it doesn't work like this. Personally, I think his life was forever changed by that encounter. I truly do. I don't think he'll ever forget it. Remember, he had already applied the Word to himself, while at the same time, denying that it was acceptable to do so.

Have you ever done that? If you have (we all have, by the way), I have a word from the Lord for you: "Stop it!" God wants to take the living Word and apply it to your personal life—in fact, He wants to apply it often, as you read the Bible. When you read the Bible, which is God's voice to us, He often lifts a word or two or a sentence or two off the page and says, *"This is for you…right now…today!"* So, the next time this happens to you, remember what it says in the Book of Hebrews, "*Today, **when** you hear His Voice, do **not** harden your hearts!*" (Hebrews 4:7, author's paraphrase).

CHAPTER 8
"PINEAPPLE THEOLOGY"

Years ago, my family and I had a sudden shift in life direction by and from the Lord. It was completely unexpected! Even though we were not fully prepared (except as the Lord had been preparing us), we grew to know that the Lord was intimately involved and blessing us with much grace during the shifting of our life's situation. In the midst of this traumatic, unexpected turn of events which included a change in my employment, ministry, church, city, and state—all of a sudden the Lord dropped this word on me: I couldn't shake the thought that I was supposed to send an article (first written in 1998) to my THE ELIJAH LIST subscribers.

When this dramatic change came for us, I went right home and penned the conclusion to the word the Lord had given me, having prepared me for this change (though I hadn't realized that such preparation was going on). For some of you, He is doing the same thing right now—preparing you for sudden and radical changes. I believe that more than 200,000 current subscribers need to read this story. Maybe it applies to you today.

Here is what I wrote that Saturday night in 1998:

Pineapple Theology? That's a strange term, isn't it? That's what I thought, too, when I was lying sleeplessly in bed a few nights ago, wondering, and more importantly, worrying about why my life wasn't turning out the way I'd planned—at least not my two-year or five-year plan. We all have times in our lives when our plan isn't coming together—or more accurately stated, when the plan has suddenly fallen apart. It's specifically *because* we all come to those times in our lives that I'm letting you in on this word I received from the Lord.

Agonizing in Bed

I lay there agonizing over one of the more major decisions of my life that had quite unexpectedly presented itself—one of those, "It can't wait until later" decisions. You know, like when God begins to change everything in your life—again—as if He hadn't changed enough things already! Suddenly, interrupting my insomnia over this issue, the Lord spoke two words to me: "*Pineapple Theology.*"

As His voice was imprinted on my mind, I asked, "What's Pineapple Theology, Lord?" But I heard only silence. Was God wanting me to explore my theology, the study of God or of religion, as it relates to the pineapple? Strange!

The Lord Was Fixin' to Teach Me Something!

I've learned not to agonize too much over what the Lord speaks to me. I knew He was fixin' to teach me something, and I also knew if it was Him speaking, He would be faithful to clarify His word. I've come to understand that not only *what* the Lord reveals, but *when* He reveals it often signifies something. So, I figured I'd leave the timing of the explanation He owed me to His discretion. (Good of me, wasn't it?) Because for now, I could make neither head nor tails of "Pineapple Theology," so I just catalogued it and went to sleep.

Last night [remember, I wrote this in 1998] I had to finalize that tough decision that God had thrust upon me. It'll change significantly the life of my family and ministry. Part of me likes it (the excitement of something new), while the other part is afraid of the unknown. The good news is that my wife and I, now married 20 years, had reached agreement on our new direction—or at least agreement about leaving the *old* direction. As always, we've made our decisions together, especially things related to following the Lord. Our marriage has been blessed in that way.

When You Least Expect It, God Speaks!

So last night, after the big decision, we went to a high school play to unwind and then arrived home rather late. While everyone was getting ready for bed, Derene and our 14-year-old daughter, a high school freshman, for some unknown reason got to feeling giddy. They started teasing and then Derene chased Danielle down the hall and into the master bedroom, where a raucous pillow fight ensued. I heard playful screaming and the thuds of pillows and then out-of-control laughter. It sounded hilarious, and I walked down the hall to check out this scene for my own entertainment. They were each laughing so hard that it was difficult for either of them to catch their breath.

As I walked into the room, I discovered that Derene had managed to more or less pin Danielle down and she was stuck and they were both laughing uncontrollably. I wanted to know what was so funny—beyond the obvious. They seemed to be laughing about more than just the pillow fight itself.

Pinned Down, So God Can Speak

It seems that before I had come into the room—right in the middle of being pinned to the bed, Danielle, the one child in the family the Lord has told us a number of times would be a prophet, trying to catch her breath while laughing, had suddenly blurted out, "*Did you know that you can't put fresh pineapple in Jell-O?*" Coming completely outside of any context, this sudden fact about pineapples had undone them both and they could barely talk, they were laughing so hard. Derene was laughing at the absurdity of this popping out of Danielle's mouth at such a strange moment, and Danielle? Well, she was just giddy and laughing out of all control!

As they told me this, I realized amidst the laughter that the Lord had just spoken to me! Not just in the words, but in the deed. Danielle, against her will, was pinned and couldn't move, and at that very instant she blurted out the beginning of the interpretation of what the Lord had spoken a few days earlier to me—Pineapple Theology.

God Will Speak When and How He Wants to Speak

It turns out that Danielle had just finished science class at school about pineapples (which I had no knowledge of) and this was the odd timing she'd *chosen* to convey her newly found "fruitful" knowledge—about pineapples. As Derene and Danielle eventually settled down from their laughter, I started questioning Danielle telling her that God was actually speaking to me through this. She explained that her science teacher had said that nobody has ever eaten fresh pineapple with Jell-O.

What? That's right.

People have eaten pineapple-flavored Jell-O, and they've eaten Jell-O made from canned pineapples, but no one has eaten fresh pineapple within Jell-O. And the reason that can be said with certainty is that fresh pineapple will not "gel" in Jell-O. It can't be done!

I went to the Internet to research it for myself and found that it's true. It turns out that the process of making canned pineapple takes the protease (enzyme) in the real pineapple and completely denatures it by the heat involved in canning. In short, the enzymes (the substance that speeds up chemical reactions) are altered and made of none effect, so canned pineapples don't interfere with the gelling process—and that's how you get pineapple Jell-O. However, if you don't cook the pineapple, but rather, put it fresh into Jell-O, the enzymes in the *fresh* pineapple simply won't allow the Jell-O to gel. Period. That's why you've never eaten fresh pineapple within Jell-O Which brings us to "Pineapple Theology."

So, what is God saying here? Let me tell you what I heard.

God's Way or My Way?

Question: Do you want the real thing? The power of God? The healthy (not cooked up) genuine—God Himself—in your plans? Then you can't put God into *your* plans, because *your* plans simply won't *gel*.

In other words, God plus *your* plans won't gel.

You want fresh pineapple *and* Jell-O? You want God *and* your plans? Then you're going to have to have an altered, artificial pineapple. You'll have to have a God that you have altered in order to get Him to gel into your plans. Try to put God into your agenda, and it simply won't be the plan of God in your life! It will be your substitute for the plan of God.

God Knows When to Speak to Get His Point Across

Isn't it funny—or interesting—or convicting—and yes, again, funny, that the Lord's *voice* came when Danielle (and therefore, you and I) was stuck? Buried? Pinned? Immobilized? She couldn't get out of her own mess. When Danielle was pinned and she didn't know how to get unstuck, that was when she laughingly said (and when I believe the Lord chose to reveal the answer to the prophetic clue): "*Did you know that you can't put fresh pineapple in Jell-O?*"

Pineapple Theology isn't something you are supposed to have or not have. It's a reality that exists by the will of God. You can't mix God's plan with yours and prosper. They don't mix. They don't gel. It simply won't work!

Suddenly Is Always When You Don't Expect It

Just like all of us at one time or another, I wasn't expecting to suddenly make the next decision or move in my own life and that of my family's. But I found myself stuck and not knowing what to do to get unstuck.

Ring any bells with you today?

"I Know the Plans I Have for You," Says the Lord—"for a Hope and a Future!"

No believer really knows what to do when God puts him or her or the family in such a pinned position. We often just try to follow our own best wisdom, but then God faithfully and ultimately shows us how our plans *are not His plans.*

You know the rest of the story. God comes through and shows you the next step and it was something you least expected and usually *never* expected, but it always turns out, at least in the long run, to be the very best thing that could ever have happened to you. The things that have happened in recent years have been exceedingly, abundantly beyond what we could have ever thought or asked! (See Ephesians 3:20.)

But it wasn't what we planned, was it?

Have you ever known a believer who didn't eventually confess, "This wasn't how I planned it, God. It was *better* than I planned it!" I don't know what you've got planned, but chances are good that God is going to surprise you soon with *His* plan!

CHAPTER 9
GOD'S VOICE—WHAT DOES IT ACTUALLY SOUND LIKE?
(IF I HAD A NICKEL FOR EVERY TIME SOMEONE ASKED ME THAT QUESTION...)

How Does God Sound?

Let me first tell you what He/His voice *doesn't* sound like. Jesus never spoke King James English. He wasn't on the Earth then. Some want to tell you that the King James Version of the Bible is the most accurate; all the while they have to translate each sentence.

I once went to a play with some "country bumpkins" who were wearing overalls with a strap missing, they were barefoot, and they spoke with an accent. This is symbolic because, when God and Jesus devised their plan, they decided that Jesus would come from the *other side of the tracks*—Galilee of the Gentiles was called "the valley of the shadow of death."

God's voice sounds like current language, not King James English, though He'll use it if you refuse to hear anything else. Mostly His voice sounds like your own thoughts—even at Pentecost, He spoke to every man and woman in their *own language*.

Never Against His Own Word

Not loudly! A still, small voice! A bruised reed He will not break! Remember, by and large, He stayed away from Jerusalem and from largely religious or pious places that were going to reject Him anyway.

Are you an electrician? Then expect God to speak to you in electrical analogies when you dream, etc. Are you a scientist? Then expect test-tube dreams and scientific analogies. Are you a

GOD'S VOICE — WHAT DOES IT ACTUALLY SOUND LIKE?

gardener? Expect to hear about ants, shrubs, plants, roses, and insects when God speaks. Zoologist? Expect talk about animals. Mysteriously, God sounds much like *you* — since He speaks to you in your own language, which is why Peter thought he was hearing from God one minute and wasn't hearing from Him another minute; even so he *was* hearing from God. The *sound* will often sound like your own voice speaking within your own head. Only a few hear the audible voice of God and that has *nothing* to do with your worthiness. Sorry! Sometimes, the least worthy hear His voice the most. God said we would never understand His ways — so don't try too hard. God will speak to you in His own way.

Being "made in His image" includes our emotions — not only our thought processes.

In effect, Paul wrote, "If you can't prophesy something nice, don't prophesy anything at all!" (See 1 Corinthians 14:1-3.) Prophecy, telling others what God has told you, is about building up, encouraging, edifying the Church — God's people.

"*Whether you turn to the right or to the left, your ears will hear a voice behind you, saying, 'This is the way; walk in it'*" (Isaiah 30:21, emphasis added). If knowing which way to turn isn't encouraging, it'll do until encouragement comes along.

The single most common misconception among those who want to hear God speak is that when they finally learn to hear God's voice, they think they will hear it in the same way others hear it. In other words, many think God's voice will sound the same to everyone. Nothing could be further from the truth.

In the same way God has created millions of plants, animals, fish, birds, and thousands of languages, so He speaks in a myriad of different ways to His people. God is creative and He loves to speak to each person differently. As surely as someone tells you how *they* hear God speak, you will hear God both similarly and also quite differently.

This Is the Day to Realize God Is Talking to You!

Joel is quoted by Peter in Acts chapter 2. This is one of the greatest sermons of all time. It took place on the Day of Pentecost, just seven weeks after the Resurrection of Jesus. Peter's famous line that day: "*This is **that***" (Acts 2:16, emphasis added).

> *Now this is what was spoken by the Prophet Joel: "In the last days, God says, I will pour out My Spirit on all people. **Your sons and daughters will prophesy**, your young men **will see visions**, your old men **will dream dreams**. Even on My servants, both men and women, I will pour out My Spirit in those days, and **they will prophesy**"*
> (Acts 2:16-18, emphasis added).

Rather than just being for men, this prophecy was for women and children, as well. Rather than just for the young teachable types, it was for the old leaders and servants, too. Everyone would experience an amazing increase in revelation from the Father, simply be cause Jesus went to the Father. He said so!

What About "Prophesy" or "Prophesying"?

Just for the record, when the Word says, "*They will prophesy*," let's clarify what this means. First, God speaks. When you hear what He speaks and you tell others what you just heard, you are prophesying—that is, you are speaking forth that which God has spoken to you. It doesn't have to be information about the future, but it can be. It's simply *speaking forth what God says*. Let's not be mysterious about these things. God tells you. You tell others. Prophesying is no more mysterious than that.

However, this book is not focused primarily on prophesying. It's about hearing God speak. But when you speak to others what God has told you, you can call it what you will. You can say, "This is what I heard," or you can say, "I think I heard God tell me," or you can say, "This is what God is saying to you, I think."

I *heartily* counsel you *not* to use the words, "Thus saith the Lord!" First of all, that's King James language and that was not the language of Jesus. Second, if you say, "Thus saith the Lord," you give people no option but to accept the word—or reject you. Forget about it! Just tell people what you *think* God may be saying based on what you think you're hearing. Life will go better for you if you do.

And one more thing: Don't try this too often with family members. It doesn't work very well. Your family knows you. You will be more accepted outside the family or outside the city or outside the country. But in the meantime, let's just go to *school* in learning to hear God speak, knowing full well you will make *many* mistakes along the way. (Note the emphasis on *many*.)

I Just Didn't Believe It—Until…

If you didn't read chapter three of this book, this would be a good time to read it or re-read it. I was quite literally ambushed by God. At a moment when I least expected it and when I least deserved it, God pulled a "suddenly" on me. He sure has a good time with that, I think. I picture Him saying to the angels, "Hey, watch this. I'm about to change Steve Shultz's life forever with this one word." (Here you can substitute your name for mine.)

A voice behind me had said, in effect, "This is the way, walk in it."

How did He speak? He showed me a Scripture and then He quickened it to me. That which was *not* alive to me suddenly *became* alive to me. It was written down and it was in the Word, but it became the *living* voice of God to me—in an instant. Remember, Jesus said to believers, *"My sheep listen to My voice"* (John 10:27). *All* of His sheep. For the record, that's you and me! Last I checked, I am still a sheep and so are you!

Within a year or so of this first encounter—now 1982—the subject came up about praying for the sick. "Preposterous,"

I thought in my mind. This was reserved for the elders, the elite pastors who were ordained seminary graduates. Not so, it turns out.

Remember the story about Claudia and her arthritis? God completely healed her in response to our obedience to His command and our faith, be it ever so weak.

John Wimber coined a phrase many years ago that is both humorous and true, "An elder is a person who 'elds'."

So What Does God's Voice Actually Sound Like?

A few — a very few of the hundreds of ways in which God speaks to His children — are listed here:

- Impressions.
- A knowing in your "knower."
- Dreams for yourself or others.
- Visions — in your mind's eye — or open-eyed visions.
- Feelings in your senses.
- The voices and counsel of others.
- "Coincidences," otherwise known as "divine appointments."
- A quickening of Scriptures, and other words or pictures.
- Signs along the way.
- Songs that are suddenly heard or come to your mind.
- Open and closed doors.
- A sudden memory.
- A voice in your mind or thoughts.
- An actual, audible voice.
- A sign or a wonder — supernatural events.

CHAPTER 10
HAVE YOU GONE "COMPELLING" LATELY?
THE CASE FOR LEARNING TO HEAR GOD'S VOICE IN THE MARKETPLACE, OTHERWISE KNOWN AS "THE REAL WORLD"

I met a young woman on an airplane while I was on my way home from one of our prophetic conferences. I had a chance to make an impression—a "touched by an angel" experience. It was different; kind of simple. The thing is, I didn't lead her to the Lord—or did I?

Have you ever been intimidated by the Scripture that says, *"Then the master said...'Go out into the highways and hedges, and compel them to come in, that my house may be filled'"* (Luke 14:23 NKJV)? Over the years, that Scripture has brought a great deal of guilt to me, because it causes me to wonder just how many people I have actually "compelled" to come to Christ. Doesn't "compel" mean to *make* someone come in? To be so forceful so as to give people no choice? That doesn't seem to be my style, if you know what I mean.

Scriptures "Hidden in Plain Sight"

There are some surprising Scriptures about compelling that have been "hidden in plain sight" all along. Here is your first clue:

Jesus hung out with sinners. He came on the scene and began to violently "rock the pharisaical boat" by demonstrating something God's people had never seen and certainly had not heard about before. It was His way of demonstrating God's newly revealed method for compelling sinners. *He hung out with them.* He spent time with them. He invited tax collectors to lunch. He talked to prostitutes. He touched the unclean. He showed compassion for people who were *caught* in sin, people who couldn't get out.

In fact, Jesus started and ended His ministry in the same way. He started by picking two thieves to walk with Him. In the end Matthew accepted and followed Him and Judas betrayed Him. As Jesus hung on the cross, once again, the Creator of the universe chose before time began to hang between two thieves. And once again, one accepted Him and the other publicly mocked Him.

Jesus had a strange way of evangelizing. He was the most *compelling* evangelist who ever lived, yet among those four thieves, He had only a 50 percent success rate. And among the crowds, before it was over, most would seem to reject Him. What a strange way to evangelize!

Only One Way to Christ—but Many Ways to *Declare* It

Jesus never asked anyone to pray the Sinner's Prayer—not that is recorded anyway. It's not wrong to pray the Sinner's Prayer; I'm just saying that it is not written in the Bible. When Nicodemus came to Him at night, Jesus showed him the Truth—the Truth, of course, is Jesus Himself. He explained some simple concepts to him; but Jesus never asked "Nick" for a decision. Did you ever notice that Nicodemus never confessed Christ or gave any indication of where he stood at that time? Yet we use John 3:16 (taken from that conversation) as one of the best Scriptures to use when leading someone to Christ.

We only discover later that Nicodemus, after Christ's crucifixion, brought 75 pounds of myrrh and aloes for Jesus' burial. Apparently, somewhere along the way, Nicodemus must have said, "I believe." When Peter shared the gospel, even in Acts, it was the crowd who pleaded, "What should we do?" They asked how to be saved and *then* Peter told them how: "Repent!"

When Philip met the Ethiopian eunuch, the eunuch wanted Philip to explain a Scripture in Isaiah to him. Philip accommodated him with Truth, to which this royal official said, "So, what should prevent me from being baptized?" Because Philip obeyed the Lord and put himself in the proximity of someone who was searching for the Messiah—on the highways of the day—salvation occurred easily for the Ethiopian.

Even when Peter was sent to the Gentile Cornelius, he had only just begun to tell the story of Jesus, when the Holy Spirit fell on all the Gentiles who were gathered there. But the Lord had *Himself* initiated the process of the whole thing, not Peter. God demonstrates, beginning with the life of Christ, that evangelism is a *process* as well as an event. If you did not grow up in the Church, did *you* believe the first time someone told you about Jesus? Or even the second or third time? If you are saved now, I believe that there was a time when you were *being saved*.

"Somebody's got to do the hard part," you say. "Somebody's got to actually lead them to the Lord." But according to Scripture, evangelism is not what you've been taught. The classic evangelist comes into town, tells you that you've got to get it together and get out into the streets. Once again, hit with guilt, you imagine going out on a street corner or into the mall, stopping people and asking them, "Do you know where you would go if you died tonight?" If the conversation is successful, you will walk away after having them pray the Sinner's Prayer and having *led* them to Christ. You'll have that "notch" in your belt.

But somehow, you can't make it out to that street corner because it feels unnatural to stop someone in their tracks with such a direct question. Jesus related to people over a period of time for the most part. There were some exceptions, of course. Like the woman at the well. Jesus enjoyed talking to the woman at the well.

He used kindness, words of knowledge, and revelation gifts to tell the woman "everything I ever did." He got her attention and then told her He was the Messiah. She and many in the city believed on Him. They heard and they believed. But again, you'll find no record of the Sinner's Prayer in that story. The Bible just says they *believed* on Him.

There is nothing wrong with the Sinner's Prayer. Many have come to the Lord through it. I've used it successfully. But the thing is, it is *not required* for people to come to Christ. How do I know? May I be blunt? Again, simply, because there is no record in the Bible of anyone praying it. Whoever believes in his or her heart and confesses with his or her mouth that Jesus is Lord will be saved. No prayer is actually required. Check it out: *"That if you confess with your mouth, 'Jesus is Lord,' and believe in your heart that God raised Him from the dead, you will be saved"* (Romans 10:9-10).

Let me put it this way. If you had an opportunity to get that far in a conversation—to tell a person the whole gospel plan—then you asked, "Does that make sense to you? Do you believe that Jesus did that for you?" And if that man or woman, boy or girl said, "Yes, I think I do believe that!"—then they have just fulfilled *entirely* Romans 10:9-10 and salvation is theirs. You are not even required to pronounce it as being so.

But there's more. Jesus was the One who harvested or evangelized the woman at the well, right? He was the world's greatest evangelist. He told His disciples a few minutes later that sharing with this woman was His food and drink. He loved this conversation! So He began to talk more about the process of evangelism while standing there at that well.

Somebody's Got to Do the Hard Part, Right?

As He talked about the harvest that was happening "even now," He explained the reality of how evangelism works. Read it slowly and carefully, or I promise you, you'll miss it—you may have been missing it for years!

Even now the reaper draws his wages, even now the harvests the crop for eternal life, so that the **sower and the reaper** may be glad together. Thus the saying "**One sows** and **another reaps**" is true. I sent you to reap **what you have not worked for.** Others have done the **hard work**, and you have **reaped** the benefits of **their labor** (John 4:36-38, emphasis added).

Jesus was telling them, "You saw the woman at this well; she has been harvested. This is My meat—to talk to and love and bring her and all her people to Myself. But what I did...," He goes on to tell them, "...wasn't the hard part. Others have done the *hard* work. They sowed into this woman's life so she was *ready* to hear about Me. Even so, I've sent you to also reap where others have sowed. They did the hard part and you have reaped the benefit of *their* labor as well."

Good Evangelists—Reapers or Sowers?

Let me put it another way. What Jesus taught brings correction to what we often think of as the classic evangelist. He or she is the one who does the *reaping*, while others heap glory and honor on them for it. But most fail to realize that this final act of reaping was only the very *last* (and easiest) part in a rather long process of sowing and *then* reaping.

What really happens is that the sowing gets done by— shall we call them "sowing evangelists"—and the reaping is done by the "reaping evangelists." It's all evangelism. But Jesus called the longterm process of sowing into people's lives the *hard* part compared to reaping. While one particular evangelist reaps 50 people, you may have sowed into 250 people's lives with seeds of the gospel and the love of God.

In the case of the woman at the well, let's say for the sake of discussion that she was 35 years old by the time she had five husbands and met Jesus. The sowing would have taken 35 years with perhaps an hour of reaping that Christ did. Jesus was keenly aware of the process of salvation. He said, "Others have done the *hard work*." With Jesus, He was always One with the Father, so it can certainly be said that if anyone could claim *all* the credit for anyone's salvation, Jesus could, but you always hear Jesus giving the glory to the Father.

Evangelism—Who *Really* Leads Someone to Christ?

Have you ever noticed—maybe even said to yourself, "Even the few people I've personally led to the Lord, I can't claim credit for because there was always someone else involved in the process. There is no way I can point to even *one* person for whose salvation I was solely responsible!"

Good! If you have said or thought that, *great*! You're getting it. That's how God planned it!

One sows and another reaps. Evangelism is never just reaping. It's sowing *and* reaping. It's set up that way. You're not supposed to have anyone for whom you can claim sole credit for their salvation. That's because the Holy Spirit is the only One who can draw *anyone* to Christ. That's true whether you evangelize in Atlanta or Africa. The Holy Spirit does the drawing and the convicting *long* before the person gifted with evangelism opens his or her mouth.

Even with Peter and Cornelius, God was working with Cornelius first. Peter simply obeyed a vision and did his part. God was the One who sowed. And who knows who else God used to speak to Cornelius earlier in his life. Then Peter reaped—if you can call it reaping. The Holy Spirit fell on the Gentiles while Peter was in mid-sentence. He never even had a chance to make a *proper* appeal, much less call for the Sinner's Prayer. It was as if the Holy Spirit interrupted Peter with, "Enough! They've heard enough! I can't wait any longer to pour out Myself and glorify Jesus!"

Let's review. Evangelism is sowing and reaping. Sowing is the *hard work*. Reaping—what most people think an evangelist does—is easier, by comparison. Have you never reaped a person in your life, but yet over the years you've invested in many people, sowing seeds of the gospel and the love of Christ into their lives? Then you've been doing the *hardest job* there is in evangelism. Well done, good and faithful servant!

It Felt Like "Touched by an Angel"

OK, back to my story. I was sitting on the plane; my wife was next to me and our intercessor, Lisa, was sitting by the window. Coming toward me up the aisle was a vivacious young woman. She was chatting with one or more people as she walked up the aisle. I was drawn to the situation and, as she passed me and sat down a few rows behind me, I eventually overheard someone ask her where she was going. She said, "Las Vegas!" with some enthusiasm.

I began to sense God giving me a word for her. Partway through the flight, I got up to use the restroom. As I stood in line, right behind was the same young woman. "Hello," I said, "How are you?"

"Oh, I'm really tired!" she said, almost looking for a bit of sympathy.

"Yeah, you have to get up pretty early to catch these flights," was all I could think of to say.

"I didn't get to bed until 2:30 this morning," she said. I knew that meant she had had almost no sleep, accounting for the time involved in getting up and getting to the airport. I could sense she wanted to talk.

"What were you doing until 2:30?" I asked.

"Partying!" she said, with an interesting combination of pleasure for how much fun it had been and a bit of embarrassment, almost as if she was ashamed to admit it. I saw her look into my eyes for some type of reaction.

"Oh," I said, feeling no condemnation or judgment. I couldn't think of anything else to say, but I felt a real Christ-love for this woman and I hoped it showed.

"I'm a flight attendant with another airline," she continued. "We flew in from Germany last night and there were all these military guys on the flight…" She didn't fill in the blanks but I'm not sure she needed to.

About that time, the restroom became available and so I didn't see her again. Toward the end of this almost four-hour flight, I got up one more time. I kept thinking I was going run into her again, as if this whole thing had been set up by God. In preparation for that, I was listening to the Lord and I felt I'd heard a word for her. As I went over this word in my mind, *just in case*, it felt like a *Touched by an Angel* word (this is something you know about if you've ever watched that television program). A simple message. A simple word about God's love.

As I walked toward the restroom, a crowd was coming up the aisle to get in line. But she wasn't there. I went into the restroom at the far back of the plane and when I came out, there she was, looking at me! Impossible! How could she be there if she wasn't even in line? Yet now there she was. But there was quite a long line and the look on everyone's face was, "Hurry up!" I made an instant decision that there was no room or opportunity here to speak to her. At least that's the way I saw it. I smiled at her, said, "Hello," and returned to my seat.

Flight Over, Opportunity Past

As we got off the plane to await our connecting flight, the three of us regrouped in an effort to decide what to eat and what to do. We had about 30 minutes to kill before getting back on the plane. I remember thinking that this woman was now long gone and I knew I'd never see her again. I wondered silently to myself and the Lord if I'd somehow missed this opportunity through disobedience.

The three of us looked in a few stores for about 10-15 minutes and then it was almost time to get back to the gate. My wife wanted to go into one more store, and Lisa wanted to go into another one across the walkway. I was finished, so they departed. After a few seconds, I realized I'd forgotten to tell Lisa I would meet them at the gate. As I crossed the busy corridor toward Lisa, I suddenly caught sight of this same woman, standing in the middle of the walkway, looking a bit lost. I hesitated and then decided to talk myself out of it again. (Ever done that?)

I changed direction, headed over to Lisa, and then I noticed that the woman had changed direction and was walking toward me, though she didn't seem to see me. I gave my message to Lisa and started back down the corridor. Now she had changed directions again to go the same way, but she still didn't seem to see me. This was getting weird. I was finally beginning to see that this was no coincidence. (I can be pretty thick, huh?) As I walked forward a bit, she stopped again over to the side, as if she was lost.

No Avoiding It, This Was God!

OK, no avoiding it, this was in fact God talking to me. I walked over to her. I thought I might have gotten the name Amber from the Lord and I'm all for *practicing*, so I figured it would be an opener, even if I was wrong.

"Hi again," I said, "your name isn't Amber, is it?"

"No," she said kindly.

"Oh, OK. Well, we talked on the plane and now I keep passing you and I feel the Lord wants me to tell you something."

Her eyes were suddenly alert, not open enough to show excitement, but yet focused on what I was about to say. "I just want to tell you that the Lord really approves of you. "A very slight smile formed on her face. "He doesn't approve of everything you do. But He *really* approves of *you* and He loves you."

Now her expression changed to show a little relief. She said, "Thank you. That really helps." And her eyes glassed over, as if she were close to tears.

"Anyway, I just wanted to tell you that you are 'marked' by God," I continued. "God has His eye on you and He has marked you. I wanted to encourage you to keep your eyes open to what He is going to *do*, because He's really watching you. He really loves you! OK?"

She nodded ever so slightly.

I moved a step back to give her space, as I could see she was a little embarrassed and didn't know what to say after that. I said, "God bless you!" She nodded and smiled, and with those glassy eyes, headed down the moving walkway, pulling her wheeled suitcase behind her. I wondered what I would see, if I could watch her expression as she walked away.

But Was It Evangelism?

There were no bells and whistles. Like I said, it was just like one of those "Touched by an Angel" episodes when the angel gets to tell a person in need, who may feel they deserve no love, that, "God loves you!" No Sinner's Prayer. No presentation of the gospel. Just sowing seeds—seeds of kindness and of God's love. And to think God cared enough to give a "lost" person that message *through me*? Wow! Many of you do something similar every day at the office or in the grocery store. Some just say a kind word to someone behind the counter or in the lunchroom. After all, every good and perfect gift and word comes down from Heaven!

For all I know, I could have been the first person who has ever said anything like that to her. And it may take ten more such encounters before she makes her move toward God. Or I may have been the "last straw." Maybe she prayed the night before to know if God was real? Maybe that's what she meant by, "Thank you; that helps."

She was found on the *highways*. But from God's point of view, knowing her heart, she might have been as far as the *hedges* surrounding the Kingdom of God. She might have been peeking over the hedges for quite some time. That's why we are told to go to the highways and along the hedges. Some are just peeking over the hedges.

I suppose someday, someone will officially "lead her to Christ" and hopefully that person will understand that there were a lot of people who played an important role in her final decision. But God already knows who they are—all of them.

"Toward" or "To"—Does It Really Matter?

In actuality I led her *toward* Christ. And isn't leading someone *toward* Christ the same as leading them *to* Christ? I think it is. I'll bet when you have shared the love of Christ like that, or you've just shown kindness in a hundred different ways—you may have never thought of it as hearing God's voice and "leading someone to Christ." But it is! And that is what Jesus called the *hard work*.

To this day, I've imagined that this young woman might have told her girlfriend about how she was bragging to some bald guy about partying, and he told her that, "The Lord approves of you. He doesn't approve of everything you do, but He approves of you and He *loves you*."

And I think her friend might have said, "You know, that just sounds a little bit too weird for me."And maybe she told her friend, "Well, I don't know. It seemed—well, it somehow seemed *compelling!*"

CHAPTER 11

HEARING GOD SPEAK THROUGH YOUR "FATHER FILTER"

Jesus gave them this answer: "I tell you the truth, the Son can do nothing by Himself; He can do only what He sees His Father doing, because whatever the Father does the Son also does"(John 5:19).

Not that many years ago, the Lord began talking to me about "the Father *filters*" I had. Now, because God is a personal Father Himself, and His plans for you and me are good, He wants to spend lots of one-on-one time with each of us. The trouble is—or was (and probably with you, too)—that I had filters in my mind that were trying to block out my heavenly Father's true voice. I just didn't know it at the time, but I would soon know it because God's intentions were that His and my relationship would get better and better.

In the meantime...

Dream On—Really!

In 1984 I'd had the first of many dreams that I would remember as coming true—though it would be five years before I would see proof of its fulfillment. We lived in Loma Linda, California, at the time, and one day I told my friend Patrick, "Last night I dreamed that you were living in Texas and you were working full-time for a Christian radio station." As it was, he was working in San Bernardino, California, in a business office.

For the sake of your curiosity, I'll get right to the conclusion of the dream and the related story. Almost five years later, Patrick and his wife, Claudia, were living in Texas, where Patrick worked fulltime in a Christian radio station! Beyond that, and unrelated to the dream, within a year of Patrick and Claudia's move to Texas, my wife and I also moved close to Texas, due to my own job transfer with a different company.

God was continuing to show Derene and me that He is always speaking to us—just as He constantly does with *all* of His children— not just preparing people for their destinies and not just keeping them on track (though that's a significant part)— but more importantly, He is building a *personal* relationship with each one of us. He does this one clue at a time, one dream at a time, or one impression at a time. Some may be more obvious than another, but eventually we realize that we have been *led all along* as to what we should or shouldn't do, where we should or shouldn't go, ways to stay out of trouble, or how to help someone. He even wants to show us where we should live.

"Proof?" you ask. OK...

Even the Exact Place To Live

From one man He made every nation of men, that they should inhabit the whole earth; and **He determined the times set for them and the exact places where they should live.** *God did this so that men would seek Him and perhaps reach out for Him and find Him, though He is not far from each one of us. "For in Him we live and move and have our being"* (Acts 17:26-28, emphasis added).

God is constantly leading us. As our Father, He nightly deposits millions of dreams among Christians and non-believers around the globe, just as He said He would in Joel chapter 2 and Acts chapter 2. Many, but not all, of these dreams are meant to proclaim future events. However, some are given to warn us of traps the enemy has set for us. In the Book of Job, we read:

For God does speak—now one way, now another— though man may not perceive it. In a dream, in a vision of the night, when deep sleep falls on men as they slumber in their beds, He may speak in their ears and terrify them with warnings, to turn man from wrongdoing and keep him from pride, to preserve his soul from the pit, his life from perishing by the sword (Job 33:14-18).

Some people call God's voice *"the pizza I ate last night."* I was actually warned by God one night a few years back, even in a dream, that if I didn't stop claiming His dreams were caused by eating *pizza,* He was going to stop giving dreams to me. I stopped! Ouch!

The "Father Factor" When Hearing His Voice

If you're a father or mother, you know your imperfections. In the same way, our own parents were clearly less than perfect. As a result of having parents who made mistakes, we tend to see God through foggy glasses and hear His voice through muffled ears, as will our own children after us. Because God is called "Father," we either consciously or unconsciously expect our heavenly Father to act in the same way our earthly fathers or our parents did—including the mistakes they made.

Have you ever had a clogged filter in your heating and airconditioning unit? Or a dirty automobile air filter? Clogged filters are no good. We all have clogged filters—some more than others filters that keep us from hearing the Lord as clearly as we want to hear Him, that is if we've come to believe that He speaks to us at all. But you may ask, "Can't God just speak plainly to us, so we can understand perfectly—every time?" Well, yes, I suppose He can.

But instead, He chooses to *spend time* with us, allowing us to make mistakes, while He builds, slowly but surely, a special relationship with us, just as our parents did with us. That part of God *is* like our parents—and it should be understood that way. Parents *train up* their children. Jesus came and spent three and a half years teaching and training up His own disciples—teaching them how to know Him, and thus, also how to know His Father's voice better. Yet Scripture demonstrates that even more training was needed for those same disciples even after Jesus ascended to Heaven. Jesus didn't ascend from a mature church. He ascended from a fledgling, baby church. This was His intention, by the way.

Peter, for instance, had to be corrected several times. God had to at one point give him a special vision just to remind him to begin looking at the Gentiles as *clean, rather than unclean,* just such a love as had been demonstrated by Jesus when He and Peter walked together. Though Peter had seen Jesus' own kindness toward Gentiles, he forgot his "lesson." Jesus had already instructed His disciples to go into all the world, among the Gentiles, not just to their own Jewish people. After Peter got his special reclarifying vision from the voice of the Lord, he then needed to bring correction to the other disciples:

> *He* [Peter] *said to them: "You are well aware that it is against our law for a Jew to associate with a Gentile or visit him. But God has shown me that I should not call any man impure or unclean"*(Acts 10:28).

Even after this, Paul would become saved, become an apostle, and would need to once again correct Peter for forgetting God's love for the "uncircumcised." Now, because our own fathers made mistakes, and we, as parents, continue to do the same, we often think wrongly of the grace of God—both for ourselves and for others. We know so little of how much we are loved by God, and we do not grasp, even remotely, the love of God for other sinners.

So, just as He did with Peter, God will—no, He *must*—speak to you and me in visions, dreams, impressions, angelic visitations, and sometimes even His audible voice—to fix areas where we are *off* or just to build a relationship with us. Jesus did say, after all, that the Holy Spirit was being sent to us, to *"lead you into all truth."* (See John 16:13.)

My "Father Ears" and "Father Fears"

There's an important reason why my heavenly Father took me through the particular processes He did. I share this because there are lessons most people can derive from it. It also demonstrates why your process may differ from mine. Your heavenly Father will be faithful to continue to speak to you, correct you, and encourage you—because He knows your history and the things you've suffered.

In my case, I was afraid of my father. I want to be honest. He was a hard man. Don't misunderstand me; I loved him. He died in 1991 and I expect to see him in Heaven someday because he got his heart right with God before his death. But I might as well be straight up about it—as a child, I was scared to death of him! And he intended to scare all six of us kids. That was his control factor. He had some pretty major issues.

Only after I was married and had our first child, did he one day call me outside and confess some shocking things about his past that made me realize why he had become such a hard man. He had wanted to serve God, but had made many wrong decisions along the way.

On top of all of that, my father was religious to the core, all his life—but not necessarily in a good way. More in a legalistic "I'm right-and-every-preacher-and-teacher-is-wrong" kind of way. With few exceptions, we learned that, to my father, most preachers were *off*. And the more any preacher or Bible teacher spoke of grace, the more my father disliked him—and he made sure to let the six of us kids know about it.

My mother, all the while, worked hard as we grew up to provide us with a good home. I remember the hours and hours she slaved over her sewing machine to make us clothes that we would otherwise be unable to afford.

Even Though *Evil*, Parents Know How to Give Good Gifts

However, because my father never understood or appreciated God's grace, he was not a happy man. Oddly enough, (and this was the contradiction that confuses many families and messes up their "God filters") even with my father, there were some good times too. You see, he actually knew how to give good gifts.

Jesus explained it like this: *"If you, then, though you are evil know how to give good gifts to your children, how much more will your Father in Heaven give good gifts to those who ask Him!"* (Matthew 7:11).

Christmas was my father's favorite holiday. We could be scared to death of him all year long, but one thing we knew Christmas, however short-lived, was going to produce some great gifts and a few happy moments for each of us, even my father! Because of this contradiction, let's just say that for me, God didn't have such a good reputation. I knew He was kind and that He was love, and all that—to *others*. But to me, I expected to be chastised, corrected, punished, disciplined, and made to pay for my sins, because that's how my earthly father treated me. Oh, and there would be a few gifts from God, now and then, maybe once or twice a year.

Afraid of God, Yet Unaware

My wife's experience was quite different. Derene, at the age of six, was lovingly taken in by her Aunt Floss and Uncle Vic after her parents were killed in an automobile accident the day after Christmas. Her aunt and uncle quickly became mom and dad to her and have been her parents ever since. Derene, though affectionately being raised by two sets of parents, developed another fear—a fear that God would take away those she loved. Hadn't God already taken away her first set of parents? What was to prevent Him from taking others from her that she loved? Her children? Her husband? The wound was very deep and it took years of healing. So, like me, Derene was "father-wounded," too—just in a different way.

The Results of Being Afraid

When you're afraid of God, it affects your worship of Him. You want to love Him and you try to "get there," but something blocks you and you can't figure it out. Personally, that is Derene's and my story. That is, until God began to speak to me. Because He knew our particular *father filters*, when the moment was right, He spoke.

God Loves to "Pop" His Voice Into Your Head

It was 1995. We had seen the healing of Claudia while we prayed three years earlier and we'd never been the same. Now we'd heard of this new fellowship group called "The Vineyard" in Anaheim, California. Healings abounded when people prayed, and I for one was going to check this thing out. By this time, I could no longer stay with the denomination I'd been raised in. Was it my father? Not really. Was it his theology in action? No. Or was it that I was learning about a loving God who still healed today—showing me that my understanding of God's love was simply wrong? I wasn't angry at anyone, I was just being slowly, but surely "re-made."

I visited the Vineyard; and at the end of the service, I said, "I'm going up there for prayer. I want to find what this is all about." Within minutes, a man and a woman, who were likely still in their twenties, as I was, came up to me to pray. I had nothing specific to ask for. I just wanted prayer. I wanted to find out what they were hearing God say. They seemed to know what He was saying to others.

"I feel like you have this pain deep inside your heart," the young woman said. Tears welled up inside me and began to flow like a waterfall. I didn't even know why. And I had no idea how she knew because I didn't even know I had this pain. "Well, I've forgiven everyone I can think of, as far as I know," I wept out loud.

"It's not that," she said. "It's about things you don't even know. Just pay attention to what happens, as God brings things to the surface to heal the pain."

When I Least Expected It

It had only been about four months. We had moved to San Clemente and found a local Vineyard Christian Fellowship. It was one of our first few visits. As I was shaving and getting ready for church, suddenly, out of nowhere, a benign, non-emotional picture or memory popped into my head.

It was a picture of a time when I was only six years old. My dad worked part-time as a janitor in the local church school to help pay the bills. As a result, he had a large bottle of *pure* ammonia. Somehow he got the idea that it would be a joke to have me sniff it. "Hey, Stephen, come here and smell this! It smells like candy," he said.

Like any kid, I complied. The bottle was in the bathroom, and I took the largest sniff a little boy could take, because my dad had said it smelled like candy. The next thing I knew, I was running down the hall, screaming! It really hurt! It caused a pain in my sinuses that was beyond description. I remember my dad laughing out loud. Perhaps he felt bad and was trying to cover up his embarrassment about what he'd just done, but maybe not.

As I stood there shaving, I realized that God was speaking to me through this memory in *my own language* and it caused me no pain. I just thought, "How interesting. Why would I think of that now?"

Later at church, a man came up to pray for me. He talked about father issues which I had not brought up. I said to him, "That's interesting you mentioned that because just this morning while shaving, I thought of this event in my life when I was a kid when my father had me sniff pure ammonia." That's about all I could say because I began to sob. I sobbed at church. I sobbed on the way home—and for the next two full days I sobbed off and on. God had spoken in a memory. For two days I was being delivered from the life-long pain of that one memory.

CHAPTER 12

HEARING VS. OBEYING GOD'S VOICE
IT'S NOT WHAT YOU HEAR, BUT WHAT YOU DO WITH WHAT YOU HEAR THAT COUNTS

We've all been "beaten up" by well-meaning Christians and Christian leaders who told us we had to be better. Better behaved. More obedient. "Do what God tells you!" The thing is, I teach that and *am* teaching that to you right now. If you want to hear God speak more, then more often do what He tells you to do! Holiness is something God likes very much. The good news: There is a provision when we aren't very holy.

Here's the tricky part, though. Sometimes obeying God is done best by doing nothing. That's right. Nothing! But one of the most important things for those who are just learning to hear God speak is what *not* to do when He speaks.

Strange, isn't it? Ok, here's the story. It took place early on in my trek to hear God speak. I had only months before heard my first word from the Lord about the condition of my heart. You may remember me referring to this experience in the preceding chapter. A girl at a local Vineyard church had said to me, "I don't know why I feel that, but I feel there is great pain inside you." Up from the depths of my being, and for a reason that I did not yet understand, I began to weep big, sloppy tears. Was it because someone knew? Was it because I now knew that *God* knew? Or was it because someone cared? Or maybe I was finally learning about something deep inside and it *"hurt so good"* to have light shone on the pain? Was it all of these things?

Now, just a few months later, I stood in a home group, and a visiting minister from the local church felt God had told him we should all stand in a circle. There were maybe twelve or so of us. He felt next that God would have him speak what he was hearing over each of us. He didn't label it anything. He just said he was going to say what God was telling him.

When my turn came, I stood there quietly. Maybe my hands were raised, I'm not sure; but I do remember that he spoke softly: "First fruits," he said. "First fruits," he said again. "The Lord says you are the first fruits. Everything that happens to your close family and friends will happen to you first." I was so encouraged by this word! In fact, it literally carried me for months—maybe years. Except for one mistake I made: I *did* something with it. Proper obedience to that word would have been to do nothing. You see, there was no directive from God; it was only an encouragement that He was at work in my life. It was also an assurance that what I was seeing Him do for me, He would do for my family and friends, as well.

Of course, God was not taken by surprise. He knew I would learn through my mistakes and that this story would be written about it so you could benefit from my foolishness. The bottom line is that for the next three or four years, on and off, I would vigorously try to make a case for what God was doing with me—with many of my family members and friends, the ones I was certain God was speaking about. I was all over this, and I was in their face about it.

The fruit of my "doing" so was terrible, if there was any fruit at all. Too many arguments. Too many controversial discussions. Too much conflict. While I felt I was simply trying to obey, what I was really doing was *doing* what I was not told to do. The fact was I wasn't told to do anything! God had simply encouraged me and given me a wonderful promise.

Now, many years later, many of those same family members and friends have slowly but surely come to serve Jesus more powerfully and more personally. Did I have anything to do with any of that? I have no idea whatsoever! I know about the many conversations we had through the years. I know that only a few have come to tell me that some of my arguments actually got to them. But really, it was the Holy Spirit fulfilling the Father's words that brought everything to pass.

Do yourself a favor. If God promises something great for your family, just love them and pray it in. Sure, you can speak up for the Lord now and then—in love. But leave the rest to the Lord. I truly believe I may have slowed things down with some family members because I thought my instructions were, "You're first fruits, so go make *fruitcakes* like yourself out of all your family and friends." It doesn't work that way.

Don't Play Holy Spirit. He Already Knows How to Play Himself

If God speaks a promise to you, then accept the promise, thank Him for it, and pray it in, even if it takes years. One gray-haired man in the church counseled me around that same time; he did so lovingly, yet firmly. As I sat in his beach house, he asked me, "Who told *you* to play Holy Spirit?"

Wow! What a new thought that was to me. I guess I'd always thought we were to be "Christ" to others. Well, yes and no. We are to love as Christ loved, but we can't change a person's heart. We can only love a person. Only *God* can change a heart. So, to obey in the most effective way sometimes means to do nothing. Have you gotten that part clear?

Remember, Jesus said: *"If you hear these words of Mine and put them into practice, you will be like a house built on a rock"* (see Matthew 7:24).

God wants you to believe He is speaking through circumstances, "coincidences," His faithfulness, divine protection, and divine provision. Remember to let God be God. He is really good at His job!

CHAPTER 13

GOD—JUST HOW BUSY IS HE?

He was both my employer and my friend. And he understood the gospel—most of it, that is. The gospel is the good news that Jesus Christ died for us. Now this may come as a shock to some, but Jesus died for sinners. In fact, the Bible teaches He died for us while we were *still* sinners! (See Romans 5:8.) We call it the gospel because "gospel" means "good news"! Jesus dying for sinners while they are still sinners is about as good news as good news gets.

But that's not the end of the story. You see, that tells you something about Jesus. He said that He came to show us the Father. When He became a friend of sinners, He *was* demonstrating by His actions, by His relationships, by His "to do" list each day—just who His Father was.

Now let's go back to my friend and employer. George (we'll call him) understood the gospel. His problem was that when it came down to the daily stuff—about God having time for us—George's understanding was of a God who lived 2,000 years ago, but was way too busy these days for just regular stuff, such as our problems. George would argue with me, "God is too busy with important things like wars, starving children, people in crisis, and people who are dying. He doesn't have time for my *little* problems!" he protested from his heart.

I must admit that his argument seemed somewhat reasonable. The thing is—it's not true!

The "God-in-the-Box" Must Be Released

As a kid I loved to play with a jack-in-the-box. Round and round I'd wind it, the music clinking along, and at just the right moment—POP!—and up would come Jack, the clown. Then I'd do it again and again. It was so dependable. It reminds me of the way many of us are with God.

When we need Him, when we *really* need Him, we wind up our prayers and, as the music of our emergency crescendos, when our situation seems finally serious enough to bother the Almighty about it, then, at just the right moment, He will suddenly *pop* up, because if He responds to anything, He responds to human emergencies.

Am I right or am I right? Is this how you often feel?

Try as I might, however, I couldn't make George understand that God cares about even the little things in our lives. I didn't have to make this up. It's in the Word of God. I especially love the Amplified version of this Scripture:

> "... *for He [God] Himself has said, I will not in any way fail you nor give you up nor leave you without support. [I will] not, [I will] not, [I will] not in any degree leave you helpless nor forsake nor let [you] down [relax My hold on you]! [Assuredly not!]" [Joshua 1:5.]*
> (Hebrews 13:5, AMP).

What Does God Have Time For?

Perhaps one of the funniest things we think about God, or the funniest *two* things we think about God, are completely contradictory thoughts. First, we say to ourselves, "God has no time for my little worries and concerns because *He's just too busy* taking care of starving children, accident victims, and wars around the world!" But at the same time, we say to ourselves—or we believe in our hearts that, "God has more than enough time to record every wrong thought and every wrong action, and every word I shouldn't have said, and I will be accountable for them some day!"

Now maybe it's just me, but it seems that you can't have it both ways. Either He's too busy for you—or He's not! David figured out *His* God wasn't too busy when he passionately penned what the Holy Spirit was speaking to him in the following Scripture:

> *O LORD, You have searched me and You know me. You know when I sit and when I rise; you perceive my thoughts from afar. You discern my going out and my lying down; You are familiar with all my ways. Before a word is on my tongue You know it completely, O LORD. You hem me in—behind and before; You have laid Your hand upon me. Such knowledge is too wonderful for me* (Psalm 139:1-6).

Then David adds, *"Where can I flee from Your presence?"* (Psalm 139:7).

You can't ever run from Him—even if you try really hard! He knows everything you do. He knows everything you're about to do. And He knows everything you're about to say! He knows all this before you do it or say it. No wonder David couldn't grasp it.

During War, God Answers Prayers—for Everyone

Jesus gave us His amazing model prayer, which included, "Give us this day, our daily bread." Now that's instruction for each person, each day, to pray for their daily bread. That's specific. I have this picture in my head. It was during the second war in Iraq. Whether the war was right or wrong, the picture in my head was of American servicemen bowing their heads and praying the Lord's Prayer out loud, while the camera recorded the action:

GOD—JUST HOW BUSY IS HE?

*"Our Father, who art in Heaven," they prayed.
"Hallowed be Thy name..."*

As they continued to pray, what they and perhaps few others fully comprehended was that they were asking God to involve Himself in answered prayers for the *entire earth*!

You know how it goes. *"Your Kingdom come. Your will be done, ON EARTH, just as it is done in Heaven!"* (author's paraphrase).

We have been taught by the Lord to pray every time we pray for God's will to be done throughout the earth. So while those soldiers probably felt they were just praying for their own safety and a swift end to the war, what they were really praying was:

- Keep all the babies safe who are being born around the globe.
- Change the hearts of drug pushers.
- Make that wedding in Israel the most blessed day of that bride's life.
- Answer the heart cry of that Iraqi mother who is asking for her son's safety.
- Take care of my mother's brother who is in the cancer ward.
- There's a little girl in Switzerland praying for a new red tricycle. Please meet her need to have faith in you.
- There are wicked people who must be caught and punished. Apprehend them.
- There are innocent people who are being forced to fight. Do not punish them.
- Bring salvation to people throughout Europe during this hour.
- Stop all the pornography being perpetrated on the Internet.
- And, oh yes, my right leg is aching, could you do something about that?
- And on and on it goes...

You see, our God is a God who is omnipresent, omniscient, omnipotent, omni-caring, and omni-everything else. He knows the number of hairs on your head, and Jesus wasn't kidding when He told us that. He knows when your mother will go home to be with the Lord and He cares that she will not be alone as she passes. He knows every single sparrow that falls. He said so. And He meant it. Not one sparrow falls to the earth unless it's that sparrow's time to go.

Just How Busy Is God?

By Heaven's standards, God is extremely relaxed and not wringing His hands at all. He's got lots of extra time available for your problems, your prayers, and your needs. So when He's talking to you, He's not rushing. He's got all the time in the world. There are lots of things He wants to say to you and to hear from you and to do with you.

Right now, He just wants you to know that.

CHAPTER 14

"HOW GOOD DO I HAVE TO BE TO HEAR GOD'S VOICE?"

This may surprise you, but for some this will be the most important topic of the entire book. Jesus answered. *"No one is good except God alone"* (Luke 18:19).

Like the Prophet Isaiah (prophets are those who get God's secret, inside information) wrote:

> *We all, like sheep, have gone astray, each of us has turned to his own way; and the LORD has laid on Him [Jesus] the iniquity of us all* (Isaiah 53:6).

Finally, Jesus makes certain to clarify that when sheep get lost, even if He has 100 of them, He'll leave 99 to go find the one lost sheep. One lost, wayward sheep:

> *Suppose one of you has a hundred sheep and loses one of them. Does he not leave the ninety-nine in the open country and go after the lost sheep until he finds it?* (Luke 15:4).

Someone might say, "Wait, are you saying we even hear God speak *before* we're saved?"

As crazy as it sounds, yes. God is drawing us. Said in another way, when God drew *you* into the fold by His Spirit, His "wooing" of you was Him actually "talking" to you. Even before you were saved, you were hearing His voice.

Look at it this way: The Holy Spirit isn't a warm, fuzzy, ooey-gooey, gaseous mist that affects your emotions in a really feel-good way. No! He is a person. His name is Holy Spirit. And the reason you feel good, the reason you are drawn to the Father, Son, and Holy Spirit, is because He is *talking* to you.

What's the Deal About Sheep?

Oddly enough, sheep generally don't have the best reputation. How often have you heard the words *sheep* and *dumb* in the same sentence? I rest my case.

Jesus said, *"My sheep listen to* [or hear] *My voice"* (John 10:27).

Here are four things that the Lord said we must seriously consider:

1. We all hear His voice because we are His sheep. (See John 10:27.)
2. No one is good, not even one of us. (See Luke 18:19.)
3. All we, just like sheep, have gone astray. (See Isaiah 53:6.)
4. God goes after every single "lost" sheep. (See Luke 15:4-7.)

The Truth About Dogs and Cats

I'm one of those dads who puts on a teasing "shell," and complains, "Why do we have four cats, two dogs, two donkeys, and a horse?" It's in my makeup to do that; I have to tease my three kids (who aren't kids anymore). Actually, I think they've figured out that I really am an "old softy" about animals. I see a great deal of the glory of God in animals. What a creative, loving God who would make such wonderful creatures for us to enjoy and use!

I felt that way until this morning. On this particular morning when I am writing this, it is our cat, Lucy—my son Christopher's cat. I doubt he even knows why the relatives we got her from gave her a human name "Lucy." For some reason, Lucy seems to be Derene's favorite cat. Go figure! Lucy is the grouchiest cat we own. Ninety-nine percent of the day Lucy wants nothing to do with anyone. She walks around with her ears pointed back, suggesting to everyone, "Don't cross me!" No petting, no holding. It seems that Lucy is constantly saying, "Keep your hands off me!" That is, except for the early mornings when I'm trying to have my quiet time with the Lord. Quiet time is when Lucy decides she loves each and every one of us. I have to keep her out of the room but it doesn't always work.

Today was one of those days when it didn't work. Derene came in and I was simply in an irritated state about the cat. "Lucy's such a hypocrite!" I protested. "All day long she wants nothing to do with us. Now, when I want a little time to read, she wants to get up in my face and be stroked!"

Derene protested just as strongly. "I love this cat. I love that about her—her finickiness!" Derene continued, "In fact, I was in the pet store the other day and I saw a cat that looked just like Lucy. She was so friendly at first and then she suddenly hissed at me. It just made me love her more, because it reminded me so much of Lucy."

Maybe it's a woman thing. I have no idea. But immediately, my spiritual *hearing* kicked into gear and I knew that somehow God was speaking to me through this silly cat. Here's your "by the way" for this chapter: God loves to talk to you through what *happens* to you. For some that day, it was "Consider the lilies." For me, it was, "Consider your Lucy!"

We all, whether cats or sheep, are the finickiest creatures on Earth's surface. One moment we are in love and worshiping God as He touches us. The next minute, we *hiss* at Him for His same touch. He hasn't changed. Our attitude has changed! What's my point? And how does that relate to "How good do I have to be to hear His voice?"

The answer—not that good! God loves finicky people. He knows how we are made. He knows what makes us tick and what makes us "hiss."

> *For He Himself knows our frame; He is mindful that we are but dust* (Psalm 103:14 NASB).

The Reason We Need to Know This...

As I travel and speak, the single most common factor among believers is their feeling of unworthiness. When you feel unworthy or disqualified—when you are beating yourself up—you tend not to have *hearing* ears. Instead of hearing what God wants to tell you, your ears hear satan's accusations or your accusations against yourself!

Forget about being good enough. It's not going to happen—ever! Not this side of the pearly gates anyway. God speaks to us because He wants to and He likes to. So just accept it.

When you're finicky, like Lucy—or when you're dumb like a sheep—here's your "Psalm" for the day. God's "voice" says this to you:

> Like a finicky cat, you treat Me like that!
> When you're the lost sheep, I don't miss a beat.
> I'm drawn to you—either way.
> I'm the same every day
> It doesn't depend on what you say.
> Just make peace with that fact.
> I'll speak to you anyway
> That's my covenant—that's my pact!

Someone Is Trying to Hand You Something

Satan is a liar and an accuser. And he knows something very important about you. He knows that you accuse yourself just a much as he accuses you! So satan stands close by and calmly holds that bat, *your bat*, in his hand. He has no intention of ever hitting you with it. He simply from time to time says, "Excuse me, ma'am (or sir), you seem to have dropped your bat."

The next time you hear that voice, don't take the bat from his hands. It is at this point when many feel they are hearing *God* speak. Many believe God must be convicting them of their sinfulness. But it's not *God's* voice they are hearing. Rather, it is usually satan doing his "torturing thing." He's good at his job. Really quite good at it! Satan wants you to beat yourself up. He wants to remind you that you're not worthy. And most certainly, he wants you to know that no matter how hard you try, you'll never be good enough—or pure enough—for God to speak to *you*.

Well, that's just plain silly, isn't it? Of course you're not good enough! That's why Jesus came as *God with skin on*. He came to die for you *because* you're not good enough! That issue has long been planned for and dealt with. And it has been forever settled!

You're not good enough! That's why He made the point of dying for you while you were *still* a sinner—to forever settle *that* issue. Oh, by the way, do you hear something?

It's that voice again. It's *His voice*! He is *still* talking—to *you!*

CHAPTER 15

"HOW BAD DO I HAVE TO BE FOR GOD TO STOP SPEAKING TO ME?"

I have an answer for this often-asked question—really bad. In fact, really, *really* bad!

"How can you say that?" you ask. Scripture, for one thing, is simply God's voice in written form. It's His voice on pages, and He desires to answer your questions—whether you're good *or* bad. But especially if you're bad and you've failed. Through the Scriptures, God is saying, "Even when you're bad, I don't cut you off. I never cut family off!" He says, "Never!"

Jesus, who came to show us exactly what His Father was like, was always accused by the religious folk of hanging out with and being a friend of sinners. He was accused of that for one reason only: He was a friend of sinners, and He loved hanging out with them. Beyond that, there are those awesome stories about the Father's love that was demonstrated by His Son, Jesus.

Eating Pig Slop, Will That DO?

Jesus comes up with this story about a guy who demanded his inheritance before the appropriate time (something he wasn't legally entitled to, but his father gave it to him anyway.) We call this wayward and selfish young son "the Prodigal Son." God probably just called him "another one of My lost sheep." This guy demands it all—the cash, the blessings, the freedom. Once he gets the inheritance from his father in his hot little hands, he blows the money on wine, women, and song, as the expression goes.

I wonder if Jesus really made up His stories. Maybe He

knew this family and this young man firsthand. Maybe this was a true story. Is it just me, or do you find it intriguing that close to the death of Lazarus, Jesus tells a story about the rich man and Lazarus? Come on! He could have used any name for this story. Maybe this really happened, and He told it to us in story form.

Now, back to the pig slop…

This young man who had squandered all his inheritance found himself both feeding and desiring to eat the same slop as the pigs—yet no one even offered him the pig's food!

Just Like You and Me

Did you ever feel like this young man—so very brilliant and wise? He finally gets it together enough to conclude the following about his life:

> *So he went and hired himself out to a citizen of that country, who sent him to his fields to feed pigs. He longed to fill his stomach with the pods* [that's short hand for "pig slop"] *that the pigs were eating, but no one gave him anything. When he came to his senses* [which is called responding to the voice of God], *he said, "How many of my father's hired men have food to spare, and here I am starving to death! I will set out and go back to my father and say to him: Father, I have sinned against heaven and against you. I am no longer worthy to be called your son; make me like one of your hired men." So he got up and went to his father* (Luke 15:15-20).

Wisdom From the Father Wins Out

Now, come on! The pig feeder—the Prodigal Son—had *a moment of wisdom*! If that wasn't wisdom, as the saying goes, "It'll do until wisdom comes along!" All wisdom—all of it—comes from God, because wisdom is God and God is wisdom!

But the wisdom from above is first pure, then peaceable, gentle, *reasonable, **full of mercy** and good fruits, unwavering, without hypocrisy* (James 3:17 NASB, emphasis added.).

I wonder if "Mr. Pig Slop" knew all along that his father would treat him better than a servant, but he was wise enough to approach his father with humility. Always a good idea, by the way—humility, that is. But only God knows what was truly in the mind of this man—or even if it was a true story at all.

You know the rest of the narrative, I'm sure.

Not only does the father, who represents God (our heavenly Father), put the thought into the young man's head to return home (that's God's voice at work, by the way), but the father kills the fatted calf and has a huge party for his staff and friends to celebrate his son's return home.

Peter—the Ultimate Failure

Just before Jesus was crucified, Peter bragged to Jesus, and he meant it from his heart, that though others might forsake Christ, he (Peter) would be willing to both fight and die for Him. However, Jesus, being the living voice of God responded by prophesying to Peter: *"Then Jesus answered, 'Will you really lay down your life for Me [Peter]? I tell you the truth, before the rooster crows, you will disown Me three times!'"* (John 13:38).

Jesus' words came true, of course, and that very thing happened, just as Jesus prophesied it would. Yet, we never hear or see so much as an "I'm sorry" coming from Peter! Nevertheless, we see just after the Resurrection, an angel, prompted by God, give this message to a few disciples at the empty tomb:

> *"Don't be alarmed," he* [the young man dressed in white] *said."You are looking for Jesus the Nazarene, who was crucified. He has risen! He is not here. See the place where they laid Him. But go; tell his disciples **and Peter**, 'He is going ahead of you into Galilee. There you will see Him, just as He told you'"*
> (Mark 16:6-7).

Have You Ever Betrayed Christ?

We have all betrayed Christ—every man, woman, and child. And when we do, Jesus makes another appointment to meet with us. You see, He just wants to talk to us. He's a relational God and a relational Father.

Have you fallen and fallen hard? Even many times, like Peter did? Then here's your answer:

Jesus, God, and the Holy Spirit, any one or all members of the Trinity—the Godhead—have a message for you: *"I'm going ahead of you. I'll be out in front. So you've recently fallen? Let's get together and have lunch. I have so much to talk to you about!"*

CHAPTER 16

DREAMS, A WAY TO HEAR GOD'S VOICE

Unclean Soap

I heard satan's voice say, "I hate the United States of America."

One night I had a most disturbing dream that I take to be a warning to the Body of Christ worldwide; and specifically, as I saw in the dream, the Body of Christ in the United States of America is mentioned and warned. The enemy of our souls has innumerable plans for countries, families, and individuals.

A particular plan is timed to be exposed now.

Without going into every detail, I saw perhaps the most hand- some man and perhaps the most beautiful woman I had seen in a long time. For hours following this dream, such that my sleep was not peaceful, I saw a romance unfold that would make any movie seem uninteresting by comparison. The man and the woman made all the right moves and said all the right things in their courtship and that had the effect of making the *story* fascinating and beautiful, romantic, and compelling.

Finally, the man asked the woman to marry him, and she quickly said, "Yes." I felt the story had reached its happiest ending and most joyful beginning. Then the man began to mention the upcoming honeymoon and the many places they could visit together. Since she, as it turned out, was originally from a place outside the United States, which I only understood at the end of the "movie-dream," and he traveled a lot himself, he wanted to take her to exotic places.

When the plans from the groom-to-be began to unfold, he

mentioned many Western countries and islands they could visit. She did the same. Then she mentioned an Eastern Bloc or Communist-type island that I did not recognize. He suddenly asked her in shock, "Which West are you actually from?" Somewhat proudly, yet not glad to be uncovered, she admitted in word and body language that this had been a huge setup to suck him into her plan—she was actually a spy who was intent on bringing America down.

Somewhere close to the end of the dream, I saw and spoke to a long-ago pastor of mine, who always represents "man's best wisdom" to me. In the dream he showed me a soap opera magazine he followed, and he showed me that he stayed close to the story lines of these shows every single day. He had many favorite soap operas here in America. In so many words, he explained with an embarrassed pride, what a large number of American Christians watch these shows daily and closely follow, even in magazines and newspapers, the many soap operas that are shown during the daytime.

As the dream was ending, I saw a clear connection between the beautiful woman and this pastor who followed soap operas. The enemy has a plan, and I heard his (the enemy's) voice say, "I hate the United States of America." His hatred was palpable. He said it so I could hear it, and simultaneously it was also said through the woman's voice to her soon-to-be, but now confused, husband.

The woman in my dream represents satan's many plans for America. Her (satan's) attempts included getting many people, especially believers in the Church, hooked on soap operas. Through this scheme, he intended to destroy many marriages in the Church, and if possible, America itself—from the inside out—through this deception. Neither I nor my family watch soap operas, but neither have I preached nor spoken against them publicly. This has not been any kind of personal issue that I have ever taken on as a focus of my own.

Yet that night, I received such a severe warning through

this dream, that I understood that through this one issue alone, many Christian marriages were in trouble and much of America and the Church in America was in danger of being led away by atheistic values—all in the name of a good story and wonderful romance that seem to be innocent and beautiful. I also had a strong sense that many who are praying for healing in their marriages will never see that healing as long as they cling to these demonically inspired "soaps."

I have no idea how many Christian men, women, and even pastors watch soap operas, but I do believe that the Lord this day is issuing a warning and explaining to all that satan's hatred for America is not manifesting mainly through open and blatant terrorism; rather, it's coming through something that has been here for decades and is much more sinister—addiction to daily soap operas, a form of soap that is indeed unclean.

*"Who the Lord **loves**, He disciplines"*(See Proverbs 3:12 and Hebrews 12:6).

My Dream About the President

As I went to sleep another night, I asked the Lord to speak to me prophetically in my dream life. Just before the sun came up in the morning, I woke up, having had the following profound dream:

In the dream, I'd been hired to work at the White House. I guess I was a new recruit. My job was to be a writer of press releases for the media on behalf of the White House. My first assignment was to write a press release about a change in the president's cabinet that involved a new cabinet member. There was a woman speech writer who had just been hired to work for the White House, as well.

I realized that significant and sudden staff changes were hap- pening within the president's staff. This new speech writer commented to someone (I overheard her) about how easy it was for her to write, as the words just came quickly. I found myself thinking that was how I felt too—as a writer. The change in staff that I needed to write a news release about was communicated to me and I began to quickly compose the press release. It went something like this:

"The White House announces a change in the president's cab- inet. Colin Powell will be leaving his position and he will be replaced by _____." I literally placed a line there because I did not yet know who the replacement would be, but I felt it would be a woman. I asked several people at the White House for some biographical information on Colin Powell for the press release, but was told it was now my job to gather that information, so I knew I had my work cut out for me.

During the next scene in the dream, the president was sitting alongside a parade route with many people passing by. The parade was not completely traditional but was more like people filing by in large numbers. A woman rode by on a horse and, when she saw that the president was there on the curb, she shouted back at her husband, who was a number of yards behind her, exclaiming, "Here's the president!" Then she pointed out where the president was sitting. We suddenly "felt" that the president was in danger for his life and I, along with a group of Secret Service and White House staffers, whisked him away, hiding him behind a nearby tree for protection.

We examined the woman's husband and, after a few minutes, decided that he was more-or-less OK. We walked him back to his car, but at the moment we got to his car, which was still close to the president, we suddenly realized it was rigged to blow up and kill as many people as possible, including the president.

At that point, I awoke from my dream.

I got up and told my wife my dream. Then I went back to bed and immediately put on my headphones, which were connected to the news, so I could hear what the breaking news might be. The very first thing I heard, as if an unseen director had shouted, "Action," was dramatic "breaking news" music, and a male voice announcing loudly, "Breaking news. Colin Powell has just resigned as Secretary of State." Then they began to postulate about who would take his place, and one of the theories was that Condoleezza Rice would be the next Secretary of State.

Later that day, it was announced that this was, in fact, the case.

Why the Dream?

First, I believe that my dream about being the one to write press releases for the White House has to do with those prophetic voices who see ahead of time what God is saying and doing.

But *timing is everything*! The timing of the Colin Powell announcement—just minutes after my dream—is the key to the second part of the dream. The first part is just to confirm the second part. You see, it was no shock that Colin Powell *might* resign. It had been talked about for weeks, if not months. But the very specific nature of my dream minutes before it actually occurred is what gives credence to the second part of the dream, which is that, as those who pray, we *must* watch and pray over the safety of our president and all our leaders.

As followers of Christ, we can simply pray and break evil spirits in the name of Jesus, and we can ask the Lord to protect our president and *all* our leaders at the federal, state, and local levels. Even the leaders in our own churches. So, take this as a call to the Body of Christ to pray to break a murderous or assassinating spirit and to speak protection and *life* over *all* of our leaders.

Blessings and protection to you all as you pray in obedience to the word of many prophets.

CHAPTER 17

WHEN THEY TELL YOU GOD DOESN'T SPEAK TODAY

I'll never forget one particular day during my freshman year in college. To say that the Christian college I attended was conservative would be an understatement. My morning class had something to do with music appreciation, though I've long since blocked out the name of the class.

The day's exercise was to take our very small group into the "Memorial Auditorium" (actual name deleted to "protect the innocent") for a music demonstration. I remember thinking that our young female professor was pretty cool, closer to our age than most professors. She was, while cool, more educated in music, and it was her job to teach us the value of *real* vs. not-so-real music. The pipe organ in that place was amazing and that's why we were there. It was the early '70s, in the midst of the Jesus Movement—or was that the hippie movement—music was changing and I suppose that's why it was decided we students needed to learn what *pure godly music* was, or wasn't.

Learning the Value of the Real

The older professor of music first demonstrated what God's music was by letting loose on the pipe organ some of the most amazing, awe-inspiring Bach, or Beethoven, or whatever it was. Wow! Who could or would deny that this music had been inspired by God. It was beautiful. It was not my style, of course, I was 19 years old. But the organ player made the pipe organ fill the room with music at ear-piercing levels—who wouldn't be impressed? When he was finished, the professor/organist turned and with an almost-smug smile, showed his pleasure at his ability to demonstrate the highest quality of music ever composed.

Next, it was time to demonstrate for our class what it was that was *not* music, because we needed to know this information, I suppose. He turned around on the bench at the magnificent pipe organ and began to fill the auditorium with the newest contemporary sounds. Line after line he played of a modern Christian song, the kind that has about eight- or ten-chord progressions per line of lyrics, with all those "fancy" new '70s style chords in about this order: E minor, followed quickly by E flat major 7th, C minor, G minor, A7, Aflat9, E flat, Fminor7, Bflat7, and more—all in close proximity to each other.

I knew he was demonstrating what he thought was not "good" music, but I was confused as to how or why he was so good at playing it. He truly was an amazing musician! As he played with musical brilliance, something inside me swelled as this music became for me pure beauty and worship, a new sound that made the now-familiar song come alive for me.

After a minute or so of this, he abruptly stopped, turned around with pride all over his face and waited for us all to say something like, "Yuck!" Instead, I couldn't hold back. I said, "I liked that! I really liked it!" My young professor seemed confused and I sensed she would never do that exercise for students again. Others muttered their agreement with me.

The music professor sat in stunned silence. His demonstration had not only *not* worked—it had miserably failed! We loved his latter piece far more than the "high-brow music" he had played first.

It's Like When We Tell Others About God's Voice

It's like that even today as God-fearing, Jesus-worshiping leaders, people who have truly been gifted by God, try to tell their people that God doesn't speak today. They say these kinds of things: "People actually presume to say, 'Thus saith the Lord,' as if God is talking personally to them."

But, as they nearly mock another person's claim that God speaks to them, it continually backfires. I think that's because somewhere deep inside each person hearing this claim—that God doesn't speak today—the Holy Spirit is telling them that what they are hearing is the opposite of truth.

The fact is, while you are being told that God doesn't speak, and you even hear a bit of mocking about it, the Holy Spirit impresses upon you something like, *"The reason you are interested in the subject of the voice of God—even when they are telling you He doesn't speak today—is that God **does speak** and your spirit is swelling with interest to know more about how He can speak **to you**!"*

So you find yourself wanting to know more.

If you believe that God speaks or even *may* speak, then maybe He will speak to you. And so the very examples used by otherwise godly men and women to prove to you that God is silent—instead begin to cause your small interest to become a big, fresh, and intense interest in learning about this God that may in fact speak to *you*.

That's what happened to me. And it's probably what happened to you, too! And, yes, there's a Scripture for this, as well. It involves the promise of the New Covenant:

> *"This is the covenant I will make with the house of Israel after that time," declares the LORD. "I will put My law in their minds and write it on their hearts. I will be their God, and they will be My people. No longer will a man teach his neighbor, or a man his brother, saying, 'Know the LORD,'* ***because they will all know Me, from the least of them to the greatest,*** *declares the LORD"* (Jeremiah 31:33-34).

Some People Have to Take Their Glasses Off to See Better

As of this writing I'm 60 years old. Now, when I really

want to see something close up, more clearly, I do what others my age often do—I take *off* my glasses. Odd, isn't it? To see more clearly, some of us have to take off what is *supposed* to help us see better!

When we learn that God did speak, has spoken, will speak, does speak, and is speaking today, the way to get closer to it is to take your eyes off the *focus* you used to have on the subject. You have to focus more closely on what you used to be unable to see. For some, it's time to take your old glasses off so you can see better. It's time to put aside some old teachings, so you can hear more clearly. It's time to take off those protective gloves, so you can feel His presence with increased sensitivity.

In other words, stay in the Word of God—but that sometimes means to do and believe exactly opposite of what you've believed before. What this means mostly is that there are voices, impressions, and clues God has been giving to you—but you've been ignoring them. It's *not* that God is *now* going to start to speak for the first time to you. No, not at all! It's that you're going to start to listen for the first time to what God has been saying to you *all along*.

And that's the subject of our next section on the many different ways God is and has been speaking to you! I call it "Debugging the Prophetic."

CHAPTER 18
DEBUGGING THE PROPHETIC

As I travel around the country, I am often asked many questions about the prophetic realm. I receive so many questions, in fact, that I feel compelled to *debug the prophetic*. In other words, I need to help people break through some of the confusion that surrounds prophetic ministry. If there is one person with such a question, there are probably hundreds who have that same question. In concluding this book, therefore, I will try to help you debug the prophetic.

Question #1: Isn't a true prophet called to point out sin in the church? And how do I know if a word I give or receive is from God?

Answer: These are the two most common questions and the easiest ones to trip or stumble over, far more than any other prophetic questions in the New Testament era. But before I address them, let's take a look at a major point or two:

1. There are as many kinds of prophetic "downloads" that are revelations from the heavenlies as there are personalities on this planet. So there is no *one* form of delivery that can be discerned as from God or not from God. We have a glimpse of this truth in First Corinthians chapter 14:

> "*...everyone who prophesies speaks to men for their strengthening, encouragement and comfort*"
> (1 Corinthians 14:3).

Now there's another concept in the prophetic that makes discerning a prophetic word properly difficult:

DEBUGGING THE PROPHETIC

2. Whether the Lord gives you a dream, a vision, a visitation, or some other type of *seer* experience with revelation included, *He often neglects to tell you if something you see, which is bad, is from the devil and is planned, is from God and is planned, or if you have the ability to stop it through prayer.*

When I first got into writing THE ELIJAH LIST, I would often receive words from people such as: "America (or the Church) was a 'stench in the nostrils of God.'" That became a key phrase that told me that the person who sent it was not acting in accordance with the Scripture passage in First Corinthians, because it was not strengthening, encouraging, or comforting.

So I began to learn (and am still learning, many years later) to discern which words are from God and which are from the devil. Let me state it this way: When I wake up with an awful dream that involves something terrible happening and I wonder where that dream came from, I head straight to the Throne of Grace and ask God to not let that bad thing happen, whether it is personal or it is related to my family, church, city, office, state, country, or something else. In most cases, I simply take the bad things to prayer and then they don't come to pass. For all I know, God has given thousands of people a similar dream and they are praying, too. This is a good practice for all Christians. If you receive a bad word, pray against it.

Even Abraham, prior to the cross and prior to the time when people began to say we have *a personal relationship with God,* got in God's face when he was told directly that God would destroy an entire city. He said these words to God:

> *Far be it from You* [God] *to do ssuch a thing* [that You've shown me or told me]—*to kill the righteous with the wicked, treating the righteous and the wicked alike. Far be it from You! Will not the Judge of all the earth do right?*
> (Genesis 18:25).

Strange, isn't it, that with regard to a personal relationship with the Creator of the world, we are afraid to get into the face of the Father and Jesus, His Son, and say, "Wouldn't You rather show mercy instead, God?" And then we could add, "Lord, I repent on behalf of the people for their sins and my own sins, but please don't destroy this city for the sins of the people."

There *are* times when God simply chooses to do His will and He just informs us, but I truly believe that most of the time He is looking for a faith-filled man or woman to "stand in the gap" so that He won't have to judge an entire city or region. Nevertheless, we are left with two principles:

> 1. Most prophecy is to meant to build up and strengthen and encourage. The very fact that God is giving revelation can be encouragement enough to get you to pray. God only tells secrets to His best friends—you and me.

> 2. There are times when God has sovereignly chosen to bring destruction after many warnings. In those rare cases, we can still affect the outcome by minimizing the destruction or saving many lives.

Question #2: I've been told, "You're just as close to God as you want to be." So, if I'm not really intimate with Him, it's all my fault—because I must not want to be close to Him. Is that right? And if I'm not close to God, I can't hear Him or prophesy for Him, right?

Answer: This is another common saying—another good-sounding statement made by many people in the Church, of which we are all a part (and which we love), yet this statement is without support in Scripture. In fact, in the Bible, the apostle Paul, *toward the end of his ministry*, said just the opposite:

> *For what I do is not the good I want to do; no, the evil I do not want to do—this I keep on doing...* (Romans 7:19).

Paul discerned that after many years of serving God, he still had to depend on the blood of Jesus, because even with Christ living inside him, he—Paul—could not be good enough—

or as close to God *as he wanted to be.* As an encouragement to you, you should press on into holiness, but, as you do so, realize something that is very important. It is found in some of Paul's verses, which are just a few verses past what we just quoted:

> **Therefore** [because of the above], *there is now no condemnation for those who are in Christ Jesus, because through Christ Jesus the law of the Spirit of life set me free from the law of sin and death*
> (Romans 8:1-2, emphasis added).

Question #3: I know this person who seems to always prophesy correctly about almost everything in my life. But this same person gives prophecies about things that will happen in the future in my nation or the world and is almost always wrong when he prophesies this way. What's up with that?

Answer: There is a fundamental misunderstanding about the nature of prophecy. God has as many versions of prophecy as He has persons and personalities in the earth. For this reason, it only makes sense when you read this Scripture:

> *For we know in part and we prophesy in part…*
> (1 Corinthians 13:9).

God has so set up the giftings in the Body of Christ so that, normally, one person prophesies well over individuals. Another prophesies best over their own nation or other nations, but doesn't do well prophesying over people. Very few prophesy well over both individuals and nations. I know of only three or four people who are able to (or at least seem able to) equally prophesy over nations and individuals. It's almost an exception to the rule that a prophet or a prophetic person can equally prophesy over both individuals and nations.

Question #4: It seems like several of my friends and people I know have all these supernatural experiences and visitations. So, since I don't see angels or have visions like they do, how am I supposed to prophesy to others like these people do?

Answer: This is one of those questions that is most asked of us and addressed the most by us. The bottom line is that some prophetically gifted people have all kinds of supernatural experiences and visions, feelings, and dreams. Yet others are expected by God to prophesy according to their faith. So, let me remind you of one of the most common instructions you'll hear from us:

We have different gifts, according to the grace given us. If a man's gift is prophesying, let him use it in proportion to his faith (Romans 12:6, emphasis added).

In my own case, the most common way I *hear*, for instance, is by *faith*. That is, I practice and learn to just—at times—*know things* about people. I practice discerning by faith. So, rather than receiving by a great experience, I often get things simply by the gift of faith, which I constantly practice. That gift comes only from Jesus Christ and His Holy Spirit.

So keep practicing!

Question #5: What's the difference between a prophet and a psychic?

Answer: Let me first state the answer in the following way and then I'll explain it more fully. The difference between a prophet or a prophetically gifted person and a psychic can be stated or discerned according to three factors:

1. Source

2. Certainty

3. Simple Obedience

What Is the Source?

Where you get your information from makes all the diffence in the world. If you intentionally tap into the spiritual realms with no intention of hearing from God, your source is wrong. God was clear regarding His feelings about this:

Let no one be found among you who sacrifices his son or daughter in the fire, who practices divination or sorcery, interprets omens, engages in witchcraft, or casts spells, or who is a medium or spiritist or who consults the dead (Deuteronomy 18:10-11).

How "Certain" Is the Word?

Many are unaware that a true prophet, who is usually accurate, can still every now and then make a mistake when prophesying. In the same way, a psychic, going to the wrong source can get it *right*, though his source is wrong, now and then. Nevertheless, *one* of the ways to know if a person is getting information from God is that they tell you it is from God, and also that the information is most often accurate. Another way of saying this is that while prophesying they are correct more times than they are incorrect.

However, even if a true prophet misses it once in a while, the Bible tells you to not be afraid of that person. Just because a person makes a mistake doesn't mean he or she is a false prophet or a psychic. It only means they are still learning to hear accurately.

If what a prophet proclaims in the name of the LORD does not take place or come true, that is a message the LORD has not spoken. That prophet has spoken presumptuously. Do not be afraid of him (Deuteronomy 18:22).

Is There Simple Obedience?

We all make mistakes—every one of us. None of us is without sin, either. But a prophet or prophetically gifted person will be found to be seeking to obey the Word of God at all times. A psychic, on the other hand, will not. The most important obedience is found in the first part above; with a prophetic person, only God, not some other power, is sought for supernatural information.

Remember again, though, as this is very important—if a prophet misses a word now and then, that is not disobedience, but the person seeking to hear God and then prophesying what they hear is still learning.

Question #6: How does Christian dream interpretation and the prophetic differ from what psychics do?

The **answer** to this question is fairly simple, really. Again, First Corinthians 14:1-3 teaches us that prophecy is mainly for encouragement, edification, or comfort. What you find is that when a dream is interpreted according to one's prophetic gift, the person will be left with hope and peace, comfort and encouragement. On the other hand, you will often find that going to a psychic will either frighten a person or even cause them some sort of lasting personal trauma. Beyond that, it may open you up (if you seek a psychic) to curses that come through that psychic because of your disobedience to God.

A true prophetic interpretation may, in fact, *warn* a person of trouble, but the purpose of that warning is to keep a person out of trouble and to cause them to pray to God to stop the trouble that is being warned about.

I once heard a godly prophet tell the story of a time when he and his wife had a dream that their son would be taken from them in a car wreck. They didn't have good teaching yet, so they cried for days over the impending loss of their son. Somehow or other, God got a hold of them and told them that this meant they were to pray *against* their son being taken in a car wreck. They obeyed God and prayed, and as a result they never lost their son to a car wreck at all.

So if you receive a bad dream, and no prophet or prophetic person is around to help you understand the meaning, simply pray that the bad dream will not come true in the way you saw it.

It's that simple. Simply act on your dream in prayer. It might go something like this: "Lord, I had this awful dream and this awful thing happened. I ask that you would intervene so that this thing that I saw will not happen! I glorify you and I acknowledge that Jesus died so I would not have to experience this terrible loss in my family."

You will be surprised how much peace you'll feel when you are fully awake after that.

Question #7: How and where do you find accountability for the accuracy and fulfillment of prophetic words delivered by the prophets today? Who can I rely on?

Answer: This is a double-edged sword that would involve listing every time a prophet is correct or accurate about a word. When we do that, people often criticize us for bragging, even when the word is accurate. At the same time, people can also accuse us of *not* having compassion, especially when it's a word of judgment—so they might charge us with simply bragging that we got it right, even though people died.

We've found that it is up to the individual to decide for himself/herself if a word is correct, and leave it mostly at that. Scripture is clear that we are to *allow* (that is, not disallow) two or three prophets to speak and let the others pass judgment or discern. (See 1 Corinthians 14:29.) That, of course, doesn't mean that a vote of five-to-four wins. The Church never voted on a word; neither do any roundtables I belong to hold the *power* (so to speak) to decide definitively if a word is correct ahead of time. We are a too-colorful group of diverse prophetic people to allow that to happen.

When we post any word at all on THE ELIJAH LIST website—any word—some think it's from God and some think it's not from God. That's the way it's supposed to work. Over time, you will decide for yourself which words you feel are trustworthy for you and/or which prophets you feel have the least or greatest credibility.

I ask several people for counsel on many of the words we post on THE ELIJAH LIST, but on the other hand, I don't ask for counsel on every word. So again, the Bible doesn't let the reader off the hook. You, not just our counselors, need to discern. What if *they* are wrong, for instance?

We must also consider what I call "the riddle factor" in most words, where God may speak in a parable or about a specific date. For instance, Hurricane Katrina seemed to be prophesied exactly one year to the date, on August 29, 2004, by Chuck Pierce (one of my advisors)—and Katrina hit on August 29, 2005! We posted that word by Chuck Pierce one year to the date, and we posted a word by Kim Clement only weeks before Katrina hit—in which he said bodies would be floating in the streets in New Orleans. (Please refer to THE ELIJAH LIST archives.) It would seem to be a very low-class thing to brag about such accuracy.

And then sometimes we find that if we simply mention that a prophetic word turned out to be a correct, year-to-the-date word, we will receive comments about *not* being compassionate. So, the bottom line: Decide for yourself which prophet/prophetess you most trust and which you don't, and leave it at that. I believe this is the wisest course.

Question #8: How can we, as Christians, know if a prophecy is true when it is *not* edifying, encouraging, or strengthening—especially when it sounds like judgment, and especially when it doesn't come to pass immediately?

Answer: There are times when God has sovereignly chosen to bring destruction after many warnings. In those rare cases, we can still affect the outcome—through prayer—by minimizing the destruction or saving many lives.

Question #9: Why are some pastors so hard on prophets and prophetic people?

Answer: This is also one of the most common complaints I get, but it's not actually the truth. The hardest people on prophets and prophetic people are *other* prophets and prophetic people. There is a single and clear reason for this. ==The problem is that most people who hear or see prophetically, expect others to see in just the same way they do. That will never happen== because the ways people see prophetically are as numerous as the number of people on earth.

We have no problem about saying that everyone's looks and personality, talents, and giftings are expected to be varied. Why, then, do we not expect prophetic people to be different in the way they see and hear? God is no less creative with prophetic types of people than He is with all people. He will cause one at the age of seven years to see and have experiences when they are caught up into Heaven and see awesome things. He'll create another to operate by faith alone.

I once asked a very high-level prophet how often—when he publicly prophesies—he *sees* everything he prophetically states, and how often he prophesies by faith. He said, "I see about 50 percent exactly what I prophesy. The other 50 percent is by faith."

But, then, that's what the Scripture confirms when it states in Romans 12:6: *"We have different gifts, according to the grace given us.* **If a man's gift is prophesying, let him use it in proportion to his faith."**

Don't be discouraged if your prophesying is by your faith alone, for you will be in good company.

Back to pastors. Most pastors who are even slightly interested in knowing what God is saying long for prophets who will not act weird and just give them a clear word from the Lord. The main problem with pastors is not in themselves, but that they often see prophetic people who have too much ambition. They first need to quench ambition and then they will most likely be very open to hearing a clearly stated word.

Work toward that!

Question #10: How do I know if I'm hearing God or if it's my own thoughts?

Answer: God was clear when He said, "My ways are not your ways." But He never said, "My thoughts won't get into your thoughts." Of course, many times you will hear the Lord and not even know it. Many prophetic people think what they *hear* is just their own thoughts. Follow your gut instincts. This is your sixth sense, but that's not what God calls it. The Bible says:

> Whether you turn to the right or to the left, your ears will hear a voice behind you, saying, "This is the way; walk in it" (Isaiah 30:21).

Sometimes when you least think you're hearing God's voice, you are hearing Him the most, because you're following your *gut instinct*, your sixth sense, or your faith, in other words.

I once asked a man, "What if I make the wrong decision when I think I've heard from God?"

He said, "Son, God can do more with your mistakes than you can do with your best obedience or your best intentions."

I like to say to people, "Don't stand there. Just do *something!*" God will make your path straight. But just like a rocket blasting off, you have to be moving in order to be guided. You can't guide a rocket that is resting on its launch pad. Just move—or in this case, *speak.* God will do the rest.

Question #11: How will I get people or my pastor to actually listen to my prophetic gift?

Answer: This is easy. Just keep prophesying and do it with grace and mercy and encouragement.

Again, we are told in First Corinthians 14:3: *"But everyone who prophesies speaks to men for their strengthening, encouragement and comfort."* People spend way too much time correcting people's sins rather than figuring out a way to encourage them. Let me state this in another way. We all sin—all of us. But it's the few who spend time asking God for an encouraging word for another person who will find their prophetic voice—and they'll not only find it, they'll discover people who will listen.

Jesus, as you may remember, except for the unrepentant Pharisees, spent most of His time encouraging, building up, and teaching those who needed those things from Him. He spent very little time correcting sin.

> **CONCLUSION**
>
> **HAVEN'T YOU NOTICED?
> GOD IS TALKING LOUDER!**

Have You Noticed? God is TALKING LOUDER NOW!

Now that you've read this far, you've probably discovered the answer to the question posed by this book, "Can't You Talk Louder, God?"

The answer is—God's been continually talking to you. Even during the entire time you've been reading this book and throughout your days and evenings, God just continues to speak—to you—personally.

He is hopelessly in love with you and He can't get enough of His relationship with you. For that reason alone, He's created and participates in hundreds and hundreds of ways of communicating with you.

Here is how the LORD put it through the writings of David:

"How precious to me are Your thoughts, God! How vast is the sum of them! **Were I to count them, they would outnumber the grains of sand—when I awake, I am still with You"** (Psalm 139:17-18, emphasis added).

David discovered that God's people, every single one of them, are so very much on the mind of the LORD that if he were to be able to count those thoughts—by God—about David, those thoughts would outnumber the sands of the earth.

I looked that up (ok I GOOGLED it!); you know, about the grains of sand on the earth. It's almost a toss up! What I Googled is—are there more stars in all the known galaxies of the universe or—are there more grains of sand on earth?

One scientist finally concluded that there may be just a few more grains of sand on earth than there are stars and planets in the known galaxies. That's billions and billions and billions and billions of grains of sand and stars in the sky. And each one represents one thought, about David, by God—and by extension, each one represents one thought about you—by God!

When I try to wrap my brain around it, I'm left speechless. Each and every day, the very thoughts God has for you and the thoughts He also has for me, outnumber the grains of sand on earth! C'mon! Oh my!!

Wow! No wonder He wants to talk to us so much. No wonder He gives us dreams. No wonder He plants impressions in our mind. No wonder a friend says the right thing at the right time just when we need a word. And no wonder, at just the right moment, a car drives by where the license plate says just what I needed to hear or read.

How does He do that?

Now, if God takes the time…I mean if God *has* the time and *uses* the time to speak to you and me that much…and He takes the time to *think* of you and me that much…that's a God I want to know better and better with each passing day.

That's the Friend and Creator I want to listen to through every single "way" He likes to speak. That means, to me, He doesn't have to talk louder at all!

NO! I just need to listen to Him by all the ways He likes to speak. He's talking plenty loud enough. It's me that needs to tune in to what He is constantly saying to me.

I was pondering about all of this the other day as I was preparing to write these final words of the book. I was thinking about how God treats us as individual friends.

As I was thinking about the book and about the Lord, I suddenly "heard" in my mind just as clear as if someone had spoken out loud...

"The eagle has landed!"

I knew God meant to encourage me that I had reached a new place in Him. That He was renewing my strength plus giving me rest, all at the same time. Like it says in Psalm 103:1-5:

"Praise the LORD, my soul; all my inmost being, praise His holy name. **Praise the LORD, my soul, and forget not all His benefits** — *who forgives all your sins and heals all your diseases, who redeems your life from the pit and crowns you with love and compassion,* <u>*who satisfies your desires with good things so that your youth is renewed like the eagle's"*</u> (emphasis added).

God loves to talk to us because He wants to constantly give us the benefits He created us to receive. He wants to give us good things. His intent is to encourage us, to renew our youth, to give us rest, and on and on and on.

So, having learned to hear His voice and to know more about how He thinks, I knew that when He told me, "The eagle has landed!" — He was encouraging me in all the ways of Psalm 103 and more. And He wants YOU to be encouraged in exactly the same way.

We are all in this walk together.

So many of our "old time" parents and grandparents understood God's intentions in communicating with us. Let me conclude this book by reminding you of the song our grandparents sang for years and years as they learned these things about God:

HAVE YOU NOTICED? GOD IS TALKING LOUDER NOW?

I come to the garden alone,
While the dew is still on the roses;
And the voice I hear, falling on my ear,
The Son of God discloses.

**And He walks with me, and He talks with me,
And He tells me I am His own,
And the joy we share as we tarry there,
None other has ever known.**

He speaks, and the sound of His voice,
Is so sweet the birds hush their singing;
And the melody that He gave to me,
Within my heart is ringing.

**<u>And He walks with me, and He talks with me,
And He tells me I am His own,
And the joy we share as we tarry there,
None other has ever known.</u>**

("In the Garden" by Charles Austin Miles, 1912)

MINISTRY RESOURCES AND CONTACT INFORMATION

THE ELIJAH LIST: www.elijahlist.com
Prophetic TV: www.prophetic.tv
ELIJAH LIST Ministries: www.elijahlistministries.com
ELIJAH SHOPPER: www.elijahshopper.com
Elijah Streams: www.elijahstreams.com
Breaking Christian News: www.breakingchristiannews.com

DOWNLOADABLE MESSAGES, MUSIC, AND E-BOOKS

Visit our Website to download prophetic messages, music, and E-Books. Use our special link:
http://www.elijahshopper.com/downloadable-products-mp3-or-pdf

Additional copies of this book and other products from Elijah List Publications are available at our Elijah Shopper store at www.elijahshopper.com.

Or call toll-free: 1-866-354-5245 or 1-541-926-3250

ELIJAH LIST PUBLICATIONS

"The lion has roared—who will not fear? The Sovereign LORD has spoken—who can but prophesy?" —Amos 3:8

Elijah List Publications
528 Ellsworth St. SW
Albany, OR 97321

Visit us at www.elijahlist.com